ON THE FRONT LINES OF LEADERSHIP

Sub-Unit Command on Operations

IN HARM'S WAY

On the Front Lines of Leadership:
Sub-Unit Command on Operations

Edited by
Colonel Bernd Horn

CANADIAN DEFENCE ACADEMY PRESS

Canadian Defence Academy Press
PO Box 17000 Stn Forces
Kingston, Ontario   K7K 7B4

Produced for the Canadian Defence Academy Press
by 17 Wing Winnipeg Publishing Office.

Cover Photo: Sergeant Gerry Pilote for DGPA/JSPA Combat Camera

Library and Archives Canada Cataloguing in Publication

In harm's way : on the front lines of leadership : sub-unit command on operations / edited by Colonel Bernd Horn.

Issued by Canadian Defence Academy.
Includes bibliographical references.
ISBN 0-662-42446-8
Cat. no.: D4-4/1-2006E

1. Canada--Armed Forces--History--20th century. 2. Canada--Armed Forces--Foreign countries. 3. Military art and science--Canada. 4. Canada--Armed Forces--Officers. 5. Command of troops. I.. Horn, Bernd, 1959- II. Canadian Defence Academy

UA600.I53 2006   355.3'0971'09049   C2005-980373-8

Printed in Canada.

1 3 5 7 9 10 8 6 4 2

TABLE OF CONTENTS

FOREWORD

I am delighted to introduce another Canadian Defence Academy (CDA) Press publication. More importantly, *On the Front Lines of Leadership: Sub-Unit Command on Operations* represents the first volume of our Canadian Forces Leadership Institute's (CFLI) *In Harm's Way* series. This seminal collection is the cornerstone of our Strategic Leadership Writing Project, which is designed to create a distinct and unique body of Canadian leadership literature and knowledge to assist leaders at all levels in the Canadian Forces (CF) in preparing themselves for operations in a complex security environment. The project also serves to inform the public in regards to the contribution of CF service personnel to Canadian society and international affairs.

This book, as well as those that will follow in the *In Harm's Way* series, represents the experiences and insights of an array of individuals who have taken the time and effort to capture their thoughts so as to benefit others. Invariably, this has meant utilizing personal leave, weekends and nights to complete their stories. Their commitment and dedication is greatly appreciated. I wish to thank all those who have risen to the challenge of preparing our successors for the challenges that lay ahead.

This volume contains a collection of "war stories" from all three environments. These stories are all based on personal experiences and the respective interpretations, reflections and lessons the authors have drawn from them. This book does not represent departmental or CF doctrine or policy. Rather, it is a very varied and unique collection of personal memoirs that are no less valid. These memoirs represent a wealth of information that can help others to prepare for operations and leadership in general. They provide challenges and possible solutions that can be used by those who find themselves in similar circumstances. In essence, they can act as virtual experience for those who have not had the opportunity to deploy on operations either in Canada or overseas. This volume also provides professional development for those with experience. One's own experience in life is always limited, and we can all profit from a repertoire of knowledge that is wider, broader, and fuller.

In closing, I wish to reiterate the importance of this volume and of those that will follow in the *In Harm's Way* series. They will prove to be important tools for the professional development of all leaders in the CF.

It is a combination of continual education, self study, reflection, training and experience on operations that allows professionals to achieve the necessary level of skill and ability to lead Canada's military men and women in an increasingly complex and dangerous security environment.

P.R. Hussey
Major-General
Commander CDA

INTRODUCTION

The dedication, initiative and professionalism of the men and women in the Canadian Forces (CF) never fail to amaze me. They have consistently done their country proud, persevering in austere, harsh and remote conditions, as well as dangerous and volatile environments. They have faced ambiguity, change, and uncertainty with courage and conviction. And, despite manpower and equipment constraints, have never failed the people or the government of Canada. Moreover, they have always been humble, if not embarrassingly discreet, about their achievements.

While this culture of understatement and humility is exceptionally commendable, it does have a significant weakness. First, it fails to educate Canadian society in regards to the contribution and sacrifice of their military personnel. As such, Canadians, including politicians, are not always fully aware of the difficulty or significance of what Canadian Forces personnel achieve. More importantly, the reluctance to share experiences deprives the institution of valuable learning opportunities.

Although the security environment is constantly changing, and each deployment or theatre of operation offers its own unique challenges, knowledge, and lessons to be learned – all still offer a wealth of material to CF members. Quite simply, vicarious experience can be derived from the actual experience of others. Leadership challenges in particular offer a bonanza of professional development opportunities. There are many situations, problems and dilemmas that are timeless and transcend missions or geographic area. The sharing of these challenges and the different approaches and / or solutions by individuals provides guidance to others, especially young, inexperienced leaders. Similarly, lessons derived from specific missions, operations or geographic areas also provide those deploying with insight and knowledge, which will allow them to be better prepared to meet the challenges and lead their personnel more effectively. This sharing of knowledge and experience throughout the institution is key to enabling mission success. It is also the cornerstone of a learning organization. It is for this reason that the Canadian Forces Leadership Institute (CFLI) established the Strategic Leadership Writing Project. It is through this vehicle that CFLI hopes to create and shape a distinct and unique body of Canadian leadership literature and knowledge that will help leaders at all rank levels in the CF prepare themselves for operations in a complex security environment. It will also educate the public in regards to the contribution of CF service personnel to Canadian society and international affairs.

On the Front Lines of Leadership: Sub-Unit Command on Operations is our first effort in this regard. As already mentioned in the foreword, it is the first volume of CFLI's *In Harm's Way* series, which captures leadership challenges of leaders of all rank levels, and from all three services, from operations in the post Cold War period from the early 1990s to the present. They are intended to act as a professional development tool for military members, as well as an educational vehicle for the Canadian public.

The chapters contained in this book, as with all future volumes, are the experiences and viewpoints of the authors and should be taken as such. Personal attitudes, biases, beliefs and interpretation are at play. Readers may not agree with all the views, opinions or statements made. This is to be expected. What is contained in this book, or in any of the volumes in the series, is not in any way meant to represent CF doctrine or official policy. Rather, it is the personal experiences and reflections of individuals who have been in harm's way in the service of their country. Their narratives are offered in the spirit of critical thought and shared experiences in an effort to assist others to be better prepared when they are called out on operations. In addition, the lessons that leap from the pages should also serve to generate discussion and debate – to determine better practices and policies that will serve to make the Canadian Forces more effective, efficient and operationally ready. Furthermore, the contributions should act as a means of sharing with the Canadian people, a glimpse of the challenges, hardships and accomplishments that their military endure and achieve.

In the end, I wish to thank the contributors for their dedication and sense of duty. Although it is the obligation of all leaders to prepare their successors for the challenges that they may face in the future, not all rise to the challenge. In addition, I wish to thank the technical component of CDA Press, 17 Wing Publishing Office, specifically Captain Phil Dawes, Evelyn Falk, Adrienne Popke, and Mike Bodnar for their expertise and professionalism in turning a raw manuscript into a refined finished product.

CHAPTER 1

REFLECTIONS OF OPERATIONAL SERVICE

Lieutenant-Colonel David Banks[1]

Undeniably, first hand experience is a valuable learning tool. The lessons learned from operational service pay great dividends – they provide a body of knowledge that can always be used in the future, particularly in times of crisis or stress. I have been fortunate enough to have participated in four international deployments (Cyprus, Mozambique, Croatia, Afghanistan), as well as on six major domestic operations (the Red River Flood, the Southern Ontario Snowstorm, the Kosovar Refugees, the G8 Kananaskis, and the B.C. Forest Fire Emergency). As such, I believe it my professional responsibility to share some of the lessons that I have gleaned over the years and in this vein will recount my experience from two separate deployments – the first in Croatia in 1994, and the second in Manitoba in 1997.

The first deployment I will discuss is Operation Harmony, Rotation 04 in 1994. During this deployment, I was the Officer Commanding (OC) Charlie Company (C Coy) of the 1st Battalion, Princess Patricia's Canadian Light Infantry (1 PPCLI). I had been serving in Mozambique on a one-year tour as an United Nations Military Observer (UNMO), having just completed five years continuous service in 1 PPCLI. I was recalled early from Africa in December 1993 and moved my family from Kingston, Ontario back to Calgary, Alberta, to take command of C Coy in January 1994.

When I arrived, the company was in the final portion of their pre-deployment training. I immediately became aware that there were difficulties in the company. The majority of these leadership challenges were of such magnitude that I was not sure I could overcome them. In retrospect, I am not sure that I ever fully met some of them.

THE PRE-DEPLOYMENT CHALLENGES

I gradually became aware of several things. First, there was a less than satisfactory relationship between the officers and Senior Non-Commissioned Officers (NCOs) of the company, primarily due, in my opinion, to a bad relationship between the previous OC and the Company Sergeant Major (CSM). The CSM was a very strong willed and capable individual, who had little or no respect for the previous OC. This feeling, as it often does, had permeated itself throughout the company. Further, the CSM's relationship with most officers in the battalion was quite bad, and the Commanding Officer (CO) himself warned me about my CSM during my arrival interview. Having been a warrant officer (WO) myself in the Reserve, I knew the importance of the OC-CSM relationship. I felt that if I could crack this particular problem, the rest of the issues might fall into line much more easily than if I was fighting with my own NCO structure, led by a disgruntled and quite possibly disloyal CSM.

My approach to this particular issue was to adopt a policy of complete honesty and forthrightness with my CSM. Due to my own personality I did not really relish this approach as I feared it would lead to ugly confrontations, but I saw no other useful option at that late stage. I called the CSM into my office, and we had a no-holds-barred man-to-man conversation about all the problems in the company, about his view of the officers, of the battalion, and finally about our relationship. I laid it out this way:

> *Sergeant-Major I will command this company, but you will run it. When we are out in front, it has to be 'yes sir, no sir' but when we are in private you just say whatever you want, no matter what. I would rather have you tell me to my face what you think than to have you say it behind my back down in CQ [Quartermaster] stores or over at the Mess.*

I am not sure what he thought about this at first: he may have wondered if I actually meant it, or if I was just saying good-sounding things to pacify him. I had to prove to him that I meant it, and I tried my best to do so over the following weeks leading up to deployment. It took some intervention, and some tongue-biting on my part, and I know that at times the officers in the company were frustrated with me for siding with the CSM. Still, it worked, and in my opinion our relationship only got stronger once we got overseas. The CSM became the "rock" of our company, on what proved to be an extremely frustrating tour for the entire battalion, involving ugly fatalities, serious injuries, some dangerous confrontations with belligerents and a high level of stress that continued to take its human toll years later. I came to rely on my CSM very heavily, and he in turn kept his word to be bluntly honest with me.

There is no doubt in my mind that our company would not have been as successful and happy as it was overseas if not for him. He has since left the Army, but I still consider him as a friend, and indeed we have drunk to our friendship since that time. He taught me a lot. In my opinion we need more CSMs possessed of his blunt forthrightness and moral courage, because in the end that is really what a CSM is needed for.

To this day, though my Regimental service is forever behind me, I remain convinced that, in a battalion, the relationship between any commander and his senior non-commissioned officer is the single most important relationship in the entire structure of relationships. If it works, you can demand and get much more from your NCOs and thus from your troops. The relationships between your own officers and their respective NCOs will be better, and you will find that you have a much better idea of what is going on within your unit or sub-unit. Failure to establish and nurture this relationship will have bad effects, both first and second order, that will ripple throughout your entire organization. I believe that this holds true at platoon, company and battalion levels.

This relationship must be based on absolute personal honesty between the two key leaders, no matter how painful it may be at first. The alternative is actually more painful and destructive. This relationship can be difficult to achieve (at least it was for me) but it must be attained. The senior NCO must always know who is boss, but the officer must remember that loyalty and respect in the Canadian Forces (CF) can only ever be earned, they cannot be demanded. Only obedience can be demanded.

The second issue that confronted me was the state of training of the company itself. While it appeared to me that the organization had so far met the "checklist" that had been laid down by the battalion prior to my return, I began to realize that the skill levels were not where they should have been at such a late stage in pre-deployment training. I knew that more work needed to be done. Unfortunately (because nothing is ever simple) the company and indeed the battalion felt that they were already the victims of an overly demanding and somewhat irrational training plan. I was not too sure what to do. I discussed it with my CSM and we came to the conclusion that, if I stated my case clearly enough to the troops, they would see the need for the additional training. He assured me that he would bring the NCOs on side.

I assembled the company and stated my case. I told them that while they had worked hard, they were not yet at the skill level where they had to be. Furthermore, I stated that as the OC I was not willing to take them on an operation in their current state. I stressed that it was a "real operation," not "Club Med" (i.e. Cyprus), and that it held serious dangers. I laid out what needed to be done, including the fact that I intended to conduct an exercise of several days duration, on a 24/7 basis, that would take them away from their families at a time when absence from home was already becoming an issue.

I had very little idea how this was going to be received by the troops, and I was quite relieved when there was no negative outburst or evident dissatisfaction. To my delight, the Senior NCOs later told me that the training was actually much needed, and that in their opinion the troops understood this. The exercise went off fairly well, and I felt that I had crossed an important obstacle.

Once again, this demonstrated to me the vital nature of the officer/NCO relationship, and the importance of honesty in dealing with subordinates. In my experience, the hardest person to fool is the Canadian soldier. By nature he is a great skeptic if not a cynic, and will sniff out untruthfulness in fairly short order. He also knows exactly how good or how bad he really is at his own skills. Alas, there is nothing to be gained by telling him he is doing well if he knows he is not.

The third pre-deployment issue that I had to deal with was the manner in which negligent discharges (ND) were to be handled in the company. The policy in the battalion was that any ND, including one occurring in an unloading bay, was to be tried by summary trial. The CO (quite improperly) had given orders as to what punishments OCs were to assign at the trial. Now, in my opinion, there are few issues that raise the ire of an infantry soldier more than the handling of NDs. Every time an ND happens, it seems to be cloaked in emotion. Perhaps this is because failure to control one's own weapon is supremely embarrassing for an infantry soldier, or perhaps because many of us say "there but for the grace of God...."

At any rate, my CSM expressed to me that our NCOs felt very strongly that the policy was wrong, and that in the particular case of an ND in an unloading bay there should be no punishment at all, as that was "Okay" in the bay. I heard from the company warrant officers, who were adamant that we should not punish any soldier who had an ND in the bay, while also suggesting that perhaps we needed to re-evaluate the entire policy. They hinted rather heavily that an ND could happen to anyone, including me.

I felt caught. On the one hand, I could well understand some of their concerns, but on the other I knew what the CO's policy was, and I was (and am) very unsympathetic to NDs. I told the assembled WOs that I was not inclined to seek any changes, but that I would think about what they had said. I mulled over it for a day or two, and finally decided to call one of my former COs, an officer I greatly respected. He mentored me on the issue, and I resolved to enforce the policy as laid out.

I went back and got the CSM and the WOs together. I explained to them that I had decided that I could not support their request, and that we would enforce the policy as it was written. They were not particularly happy, but accepted my decision. Fortunately, I cannot recall ever trying an ND in my company. While I did not feel very comfortable denying my NCOs, I knew that I had given the issue an honest evaluation and sought other wiser opinion. Because of that I was prepared to stand by my decision not to seek a change of policy. It was not a particularly happy passage, but the fact that it did not lead to other problems was a tribute to the concept I mentioned above - a strong officer-NCO relationship based on openness and trust, and some demonstration of respect for the concerns of subordinates. As well, it proved to me for the first time how important it is to have mentors to whom we can turn for advice and help without compromising ourselves. I am a great believer in mentorship and have since both sought it and offered it on several occasions.

IN-THEATRE CHALLENGES

Our mission in Croatia in the spring and summer of 1994 presented me with a second set of leadership challenges, different from the first because they were underlain by the risks and threats of the theatre. We were present in the Srbska Krijena during a sort of lull, or armed truce, that resulted from the inconclusive fighting of the previous year, before the more successful Croatian (HV) offensive (i.e. AKTION GROM) that occurred in summer 1995. In spite of this, there were still tensions with both sides, and confrontations took place on several occasions. These were more commonly with the Republic of Srbska Krijena (RSK) forces but occasionally and on a lesser scale with the HV. Offsetting these circumstances was the fact that I had by this stage been able to forge a fairly effective NCO/officer team in the company, and enjoyed an excellent relationship with my CSM.

I will describe three situations that took place in my company. I was directly involved in two of these, and my second in command (2IC) and CSM were involved in the third. I have included the third because of its unique nature, as well the sterling qualities displayed by my 2IC and CSM during a potentially catastrophic incident.

In the first case, the mission for CANBAT (Canadian Battalion) as laid down to us by the United Nations Protection Force (UNPROFOR) headquarters was to prevent a military incursion into the United Nations Protected Area (UNPA), i.e. the Serb Krijena. All talk of "neutrality" aside, what this meant was that we were to be prepared to defend the Zone of Separation against offensive action, most likely by HV forces against the RSK. Accordingly, my company was assigned a fairly elongated sector of the battalion's Area of Operation (AO), in which we were required both to enforce the conditions of the United Nations (UN) ceasefire, as well as to be prepared to stop offensive action.

Unfortunately, the battalion group was not nearly large enough to carry out all of these tasks effectively, in particular due to the fact that we had only three rifle companies spread over a very large and contentious AO. The result at company level was that my platoons were dispersed in isolated Observation Posts (OPs) with no real possibility for mutual support, and I was able to retain only a very small reserve to act as a Quick Reaction Force (QRF).

Regardless of these realities, we had a mission to carry out. We constructed our OPs as defensibly as we possibly could, and ensured that our support weapons were all deployed forward onto the line. Armoured Personnel Carriers (APCs) were dug in as much as possible, and anti-RPG (rocket propelled grenades) wire nets rigged. Large stocks of combat supplies were held in each OP, each of which was manned by a section. This was all good. The problem, which my CSM soon brought to my attention, was that the troops were not impressed by the situation they would probably face if the HV were to launch an offensive through our sector.[2]   In essence, our orders required us to engage hostile forces entering the zone in order to protect the UNPA, regardless of whether or not the hostile forces were directly engaging us. The difficulty was, of course, that the combat power of the OPs was limited, and there was very little chance that any help would be forthcoming, either from other OPs or from company headquarters (HQ), and even less likely from the distant battalion reserve. In the minds of the troops, as the CSM explained, the situation was verging on suicidal.

I was now confronted by a situation in which I was asking my soldiers to do something that they knew was not only quite risky (which, on its own, they might have accepted) but also very unlikely to succeed against any respectable hostile force. I knew that I could not let this fester, nor pretend that the problem did not exist. To me, the approach of "just shut up and do what you're told" was a non-starter, and in any case that was not the manner in which we ran our ship.

I decided that the only way to do it was to sit down with the troops and try to explain to them why it was important. I tackled this by visiting each OP along with the CSM, but I did not enjoy it, nor did I feel confident in what I was saying to them. I could see in their faces and in their unusual quietness that they did not buy it at all. Perhaps my uncertainty communicated itself to them. At any rate, after representation by myself and the other line OC to the CO, he eventually revised his orders and the OPs were to fire only if they judged an imminent threat directly to themselves. Not particularly morally satisfying in view of our mandate perhaps, but looking back on what later occurred in the Krijena, and the severe lack of any robust combat capability to support our line or to deter a belligerent offensive (despite the illusory name "Protection Force), it may have been the most realistic course of action. When I communicated this change to the troops, it was accepted in a more positive way. Still, the whole business remained under my skin.

What I drew from this were two things. First, that Canadian soldiers are willing to take risks, sometimes great risks, but they must know and understand the reason why. They are not Wellington's "scum of the earth" and they cannot be flogged into battle. If they do not understand why, or do not identify with the reason, they may demonstrate a reluctance to risk themselves. This uncertainty on their part was further reinforced by a visit from our parent Brigade Commander from Canada, who announced at one of my OPs that there was nothing in Croatia worth risking the life of one Canadian soldier.

The second point I drew was when confronted with a clearly impractical order, or an order that appears to impose an unnecessary level of risk, the commander has a duty to his troops to raise his objections to the order. If he is successful in having the order amended, good for him. If he is not, he must then be prepared to make a direct personal connection with his troops in order to explain what is required of them. Just sending such an order "down the pipe" is, in my opinion, poor leadership. In my case, I got the sequence backwards and experienced a serious morale issue amongst my troops.

The second challenge I wish to recount was an incident that occurred at night in my company sector, in the vicinity of a particularly unhappy and contentious Serb village. One of the problems we faced in dealing with the Serbs was the very strong belief on their part that we were conspiring with the HV to "bring back the Croats" to the Krijena, in order to reoccupy their former homes and villages. The Serbs were always vigilant for any alleged treachery on our part, and one day the ill advised but innocent actions of one of my patrols gave the local Serb troublemakers the pretext they were looking for.

While conducting a daytime APC patrol along the Croat Line of Separation, the patrol was stopped by a Croat civilian who identified himself as a priest, whose pre-war residence now lay on the Serb side of the Zone. He asked the patrol to transport him across the Zone to his old residence, in order that he could check on his house. While this was technically not permitted, we were at that time engaged in village visitation programs to allow displaced Croats to visit their former communities inside the Zone. With this in mind, the patrol commander decided that the request was valid, and proceeded to transport the priest across to the Serb side. The priest quickly entered a house, then got back in the APC and was returned to the Croat side. While this might, on the face of it, have been seen as a simple humanitarian act in keeping with higher intent, the local Serbs, some of who had noted the visit, did not see it this way.

Later that night, I was called to the company command post (CP) as a result of an incident on the line. It transpired that the local Serbs in the area of the visit had decided that we were in the process of bringing Croat spies into the Krajina, just as their conventional wisdom always held that we would. Arming themselves with small arms, grenades, mines and fortified with the ubiquitous moonshine, an unpleasant crowd of locals had stopped the same APC during a night patrol, surrounding it and putting mines on the road. The patrol commander had buttoned up and was awaiting help. According to his report, the situation was becoming increasingly tense. Instructing the CP to alert battalion HQ, I called out my small QRF, got in my jeep (being much faster than my APC) and headed out into the night, without much clear idea of exactly how I would deal with this confrontation.

On arrival, I found the APC surrounded by a mob of about 20-30 angry armed locals, some of who appeared to be drunk. It looked quite ugly. I was able to get into the APC to talk to the patrol commander, who explained the situation to me. Since the use of force seemed very likely to produce fatal results, I decided to try to make a display of good faith. Using a local translator, I explained to the leader of the crowd that the incident was all a mistake. This was met with derision and disbelief. I realized that this would be harder than I thought. Fortunately, we were able to summon a UNCIVPOL (UN civilian police) Royal Canadian Mounted Police (RCMP) officer to the scene. The Serbs seemed to have a bit more trust in the impartiality of UNCIVPOL than they had in us. I proposed to the crowd leader that he and I and the RCMP officer climb into the APC and talk to the crew, so that the soldiers could explain in their own words what they had done, and the Serb could see that my men genuinely had no bad intent in their actions. He agreed with some skepticism, and with the aid of a local translator we commenced this strange dialogue inside the cramped, hot APC.

My troops were not comfortable with my explanation of what I intended, but as none of us could see a better course of action, they did their best. The Serb leader made a huge of show of belligerent bravado, and made a point of grilling the troops and giving us a verbal dressing down. However, once the conversation was over, he got out and spoke with his group. After some further yelling and shouting, they slowly dispersed into the darkness. Although my reserve was located nearby, and the battalion reserve was alerted, we had been able to avoid the use of force, which in the confused darkness could have resulted in a catastrophe. I found the entire incident very stressful, if not to say frightening, to say nothing of what my soldiers had gone through awaiting the arrival of help. I was very proud of how the troops had behaved in the face of possibly lethal unpredictability.

This incident reminded me of two facts. First, in an operation such as we were engaged in, the "strategic corporal" concept is entirely valid. In order for this corporal to be most effective, he (and his soldiers) must fully understand the big picture. I failed in that regard. Second, we need to train leaders to be able to conduct negotiations under conditions that are at once stressful, confused, and dangerous. Nice "mediation"-style chatting across a table is next to useless.

The final incident was one which took place while I was away on leave, but which in my opinion exemplifies some vitally important leadership issues. At one point on my company line was a Serb village whose southern edge immediately abutted the Serb Line of Separation. Located just inside the Zone, and technically in violation of the Ceasefire, was the village's defensive fighting position, sited to defend the village from attack by the HV located a couple of kilometers to the south across the Zone. In defiance of their own government, as well as all our efforts at negotiation, the local militiamen insisted on occupying the position, thus further inflaming the Croats who would make periodic threats about taking matters into their own hands. Immediately to the northwest of the village was a smaller bunker, sited to protect the flank of the village. My company had raided this bunker on a couple of occasions, but the Serbs persisted in returning to it when they thought we were not around.

One day (in my absence) the CO decided to finally readdress the situation once and for all. He dispatched a task force composed of elements of the battalion reserve, along with an element of combat engineers. This force entered my area (with no coordination with my company), and proceeded directly to the western bunker, evicting the Serb militiamen and then destroying the bunker. Unfortunately, while this was going on the village's defence company had been alerted, and the locals began to arm. After having completed their task at the first bunker, the task force then proceeded to enter the village from the northwest, with the intention of destroying the main fighting position. As fate would have it, the lead vehicle took a wrong turn and the column became stuck, unable to turn around or to reverse amid the narrow village streets or the growing crowd of armed and angry locals.

A stand-off rapidly developed, with the troops confined to their armoured vehicles, surrounded and blocked by a mixed crowd that included both armed militia (including M-80s and at least one Sagger anti tank missile) and unarmed women and children. A single shot by either side might have triggered an indiscriminate short-range slaughter. The task force commander commenced an attempt at negotiation with the leader of the crowd, but with little result. A terribly dangerous situation had developed.

Fortunately, at that moment my 2IC (at that time the acting OC) and my CSM arrived in the village during a routine line tour, and happened upon this confrontation in progress. Well known and respected in the village, my 2IC was considered a credible figure by the local leadership. While the 2IC intervened between the Serbs and the beleaguered task force, my CSM moved amongst the troops of the task force and gave encouragement and preparatory fire orders. The negotiations dragged on, but gradually my 2IC was able to defuse the situation and in due course the task force withdrew, its ill-considered mission incomplete.

The day after the incident, the commander of the village's defence company visited our camp, bringing an extraordinary gift for the 2IC: a Serb army captain's uniform. He thanked my 2IC for his efforts in averting disaster. "My mother wanted me to say to you," he stated, " that if was not for you, there would have been many dead Serbs and dead Canadians." My CSM later told me that he was the most frightened he had ever been in his entire service career. Despite this, he performed in an exemplary fashion. Sad to say, although my 2IC later received the CDS' Commendation for another brave action, neither he nor the CSM were granted any recognition for their intervention that day, probably because of the negative picture the incident would have painted of the Canadians who had provoked it.

This incident, which was happily resolved without loss to either side, exemplifies the importance of two leadership traits: the ability to rapidly assess a confused, dangerous situation, then develop a workable solution and act on it. Again, I believe that our training, both in the schools and in TMST, must be as realistic and demanding as possible. Innocuous little scenarios that are easily solved by "checklist" solutions are of limited value except as a very elementary first step in training.

Secondly, and perhaps more importantly, I am reminded of the huge value of courage in the face of danger. Courage does not mean the absence of fear; rather it means the ability to continue to act rationally and effectively in the face of fear and risk. I am not sure that in our training of leaders or even in our military culture we celebrate this courage sufficiently, nor seek to encourage it. Perhaps we find it a bit too intense or "gung ho" for our bland Canadian palates, but we must remember that the annals of our military history are filled with examples of selfless courage the equal of any military in the world. We need to have these examples more present in our daily lives.

OP HARMONY SUMMARY

Having related several leadership challenges that we faced in both the pre-deployment and force employment stages of an overseas operation, I would like to summarize the key points:

1. the relationship between any commander and his senior warrant officer is the single most important relationship in the entire unit and sub-unit structure;

2. loyalty and respect in the Canadian Forces are only ever earned – they cannot be not demanded;

3. honesty is all important in dealing with subordinates;

4. the Canadian soldier knows exactly how good or how bad he really is at his own skills: there is nothing to be gained by telling him he is doing well if he knows he is not;

5. be willing to consider the opinions and concerns of your subordinates, but be strong enough to stand by your own convictions if you cannot agree;

6. mentors to whom you can turn for advice and help without compromising yourself are crucial;

7. Canadian soldiers are willing to take risks, sometimes great risks, but they must know and understand the reason why. If they do not understand why, or do not identify with the reason, they may demonstrate a reluctance to risk themselves;

8. when confronted with a clearly impractical order, or an order that appears to impose an unnecessary level of risk, it is the commander's duty to his troops to raise his objections to the order;

9. a clear understanding of the bigger picture and higher intent in an operation at all rank levels is key to the effectiveness of the "strategic corporal";

10. leaders must be trained to rapidly assess a dangerous and confused situation, and develop a workable solution; and

11. value and recognize courage in the face of danger, and ensure you constantly develop and reward the concept and conduct of physical courage.

OPERATION ASSISTANCE

During Operation Assistance, the domestic operation in support of the Government of Manitoba during the 1997 Red River Flood, I was the Deputy Commanding Officer (DCO) of 1 PPCLI. At this time I had spent nearly eight years of consecutive service in the battalion. Our battalion received the order to deploy while on exercise in Wainwright, and we moved immediately by road to Shilo, then staged forward into the upper Red River basin, in the vicinity of Altona-Morrison-Dominion City-Emerson. Our battalion HQ was established in the Altona community centre, with our companies quartered in villages around the Area of Operations (AO). Due to road closures, Administration Company deployed into Kapyong Barracks, about two hours away. Our main mission was to support each Rural Municipality (RM) in its fight against the rising waters, although on occasion we actually found ourselves facilitating the coordination of the efforts of provincial and local agencies, who were not always working in the most unified manner.

As DCO, the CO assigned me two roles. First, I was employed as a sort of "Chief of Staff" running our HQ, which included the representatives of various attachments, as well as civilian agencies and, quite often, media. This allowed the CO to roam the AO, and also freed up the Operations Officer (Ops O) and his staff to concentrate more on planning and coordination, and less on managing the HQ. Secondly, I was assigned the role of "Town Major," or liaison with the municipal authorities of Altona.

This proved to be by far the most interesting part of my job, because it placed me in "leadership" situations where the behaviour I was attempting to influence was not that of soldiers, but rather that of civil officials. Another potential complication was that, since Altona is a pacifist Mennonite community, we had to prepare for the possibility of a rather indifferent reception.

Domestic operations require military leaders to cooperate with local civil officials and even private citizens. These civil officials, while normally dedicated citizens, are of varying degrees of competency in terms of operational planning and "command and control." In some situations, despite our best efforts we may find ourselves "leading" by default. Rather than relate specific incidents, I will offer some summary points:

1. Try to understand the concerns of the civil officials. They work with a different set of imperatives and constraints, and may be unable to make decisions or to give orders in the peremptory manner that we soldiers expect in a crisis situation. This can be extremely frustrating for us, and can cause bad relations if not managed. Patience and understanding are essential when dealing with civilian officials;

2. Be careful to manage the expectations of local officials. In my experience many of these good people know little or nothing about military capabilities, and have seriously unrealistic expectations, which can quickly manifest themselves as demands for services we cannot deliver, for practical or legal reasons. In particular, avoid illegal involvement in support of law enforcement agencies-many local constabularies (and some larger ones), who do not understand how the laws of Canada pertain to this issue, may see you as extra manpower;

3. Watch out for morale issues in the troops, especially in the later stages of the operation when there are fewer demands on them. Ensure that there are suitable and adequate means of recreation and relaxation available, or that spare time is spent in useful training activities. This problem is almost always exacerbated by the dismal slowness of National Defence Headquarters (NDHQ) in issuing authority to commence withdrawal and redeployment. I have been involved in several major domestic operations at unit, brigade and Area level, and I have always found this inexplicable foot-dragging to be a contributor to morale issues at the end of a domestic operation;

4. Take care to see that the troops are not put at unnecessary risk by using civilian equipment without training, or conversely that they are not exposed to hazardous situations without proper protective equipment, some of which is not provided by the CF and must be purchased locally. Floodwaters, for example, can be polluted, deep, cold and swift. We do not normally issue adequate protective gear against these conditions—civilian pattern immersion suits are required. The troops are full of the desire to help out, and sometimes must be protected against themselves;

5. Deploy with all your organization and capabilities intact. We have a terrible tendency to drop everything we know and start trying to re-invent ourselves in a domestic operation. Take everything, and everybody, except maybe the heavy support weapons. Almost everything and everybody we have in a battalion has very useful and important roles in a domestic operation, as we discovered on several occasions in Manitoba. If you leave things behind, you lose capabilities and thus flexibility. Particularly important are those assets that provide mobility, sustainment and Command, Control, Communications and Intelligence (C3I); and

6. My caveats above notwithstanding, be prepared to bend things a bit to help municipal authorities who are *in extremis* or who have willingly helped your unit out with their own resources. On one occasion, I refueled several pieces of the town of Altona's municipal machinery, (in exchange for their kindly clearing out a large vehicle park for us), so that they could immediately get back to the business of keeping the municipal roads open. This gesture was repaid in good will.

If you can manage to master these points of domestic operations leadership, your force will have a successful mission and will reap the good will of the local citizenry. In our case, the pacifist Mennonites of Altona marked our final departure from their midst with generosity and gratitude, expressed by allowing us to stage a cenotaph parade in the centre of town. This was followed by a presentation of gifts to the town from the battalion, and then a dinner and dance put on for us by the townspeople.

CONCLUSION

In this chapter, I have offered some perspectives on leadership in operations, both deployed and domestic. Not all that I have said may prove to be relevant or useful, nor may it be exactly " by the book." Some people, no doubt, recognizing themselves in print, may not be happy with my interpretation of events. Regardless, I hope that what I said may be of some value to others.

ENDNOTES

1   Lieutenant-Colonel David Banks is a PPCLI officer with 31 years of service: eight as a Reserve Infantry NCM and 23 as a Regular Force Infantry Officer.

2   As later happened to CANBAT in the summer of 1995 when the HV launched Aktion Grom.

CHAPTER 2

VERGING ON THE ABSURD
THE SREBRENICA RELIEF CONVOY

Colonel Bernd Horn

War stories are invariably of greater interest to the storyteller than they are to the listener - usually poor victims who are cornered and entrapped and therefore, must endure epic sagas with little hope of a quick escape. However, war stories are important as they impart actual experience from which lessons and knowledge can be drawn. They are particularly valuable for those who have not yet had the opportunity to gain operational experience of their own. As such, war stories impart a form of vicarious experience that provides situations, challenges and problems, as well as the respective solutions that others have used to overcome them. In the absence of clear direction or ideas, they represent possible courses of action to assist decision-making in a crisis. It is for this reason that all military personnel, particularly senior leaders, have a responsibility, if not a duty, to share their experiences and knowledge to ensure those that follow in their footsteps are prepared for the challenges that they may face.

This chapter is a direct result of that philosophy. Although I believe it is a good war story, more importantly, it contains valuable experiences that transcend the actual mission or tour. In retrospect, I realize now that I would do some things differently if I had the opportunity to redo the mission – that is a result of time to reflect on the events. But, then again, that is why war stories are a valuable professional development tool.

OPERATION CAVALIER

In October 1992, as the Officer Commanding (OC) Bravo Company ("B" Coy) of the 1st Battalion, The Royal Canadian Regiment (1 RCR), my company was attached to the 2 RCR Battle Group (BG), which was selected for Rotation (Roto) 0, of Operation (Op) Cavalier, the Canadian deployment to Bosnia-Herzegovina (BH). The BG initially deployed to Croatia, and after several frustrating months of negotiations, it finally moved in late February 1993 to its operational bases in Visoko and Kiseljak, BH. Once on the ground in BH, the 2 RCR BG immediately began to undertake a variety of missions from humanitarian convoy escorts to infrastructure repair tasks in Sarajevo.

WARNING ORDER

On 9 March 1993, the Battle Group headquarters (HQ) received a warning order to escort a UN High Commission for Refugees (UNHCR) convoy carrying humanitarian supplies to Srebrenica, an isolated mining town located in a steep-sloped valley in south-eastern Bosnia. The besieged Muslim enclave had been surrounded and cut-off by Serb forces for over eight months. Apparently, the last time a humanitarian aid convoy delivered aid to Srebrenica (10 December 1992), the entrapped forces launched an offensive in the immediate aftermath of the food delivery. As a result, justifiably or not, the besieging Serb army equated food aid, or at least the arrival of humanitarian convoys, with combat capability.

Nonetheless, the mission was passed to me and my sub-unit. The "B" Coy (minus) force was to rendezvous with a UNHCR convoy from Belgrade at Banja Kobiljaca and escort them to Srebrenica and back.[1] BH Command estimated that the mission would last only three days. Our BG HQ cautioned us that it would probably take four to five days and I "cleverly" warned off my team that I thought we would be on the road for at least seven to ten days. We were all wrong. Although not evident at the time, the haphazard and disorganized initiation of the mission foreshadowed its later chaotic execution.

We received the warning order late in the morning and we were expected to be at the Sarajevo airport that night for an early departure the next morning. Our HQ had no information on routes, threats, liaison officers, when our attachments would arrive, or any other detailed information. A visit to BH Command in Kiseljak was of marginal value, however, it did support the normal clichés of dealing with higher headquarters. When I spoke with the head of convoy operations I mentioned I would need a guide to take us through the Sarajevo airport in accordance with the BH Command standard operating procedures (SOPs) early the next morning. He promptly blew me off stating that there was "not enough time lead-up" and that he would "need more notice."[2] I replied that the lack of notice was due to the fact that we had just received warning of the mission mere hours ago. He sympathized but reaffirmed, "yes, but we need more notice."

Totally perplexed, in the end, I was assured by the Chief of Staff (COS) we would have our guide. It appeared that French Lieutenant-General Philippe Morillon, Commander of UN Forces in BH, had a vested interest in our task. In fact, he would accompany the convoy into the pocket. As a result, BH Command would graciously overlook "our" failure to provide adequate notice and provide us with the needed guides.

Back at our base camp, preparations were well under way. Fuel now became a problem – our administrative company had no fuel for us – and as far as they were concerned it now became a "personal problem" for us to solve. We scrounged every available jerry can in camp when all of a sudden a fuel bowser appeared to fill our requirement. Despite the challenges, the "B" Coy escort, including attachments, were ready at 1900 hours that night.

WELCOME TO THE CIRCUS

We departed at 0550 hours, on 10 March. The slow underpowered M-113 armoured personnel carriers (APCs), combined with the steep, narrow mountainous roads and numerous checkpoints throughout the entire route turned the 230 kilometre (km) trip into a 12 hour ordeal. We arrived at the rendezvous at 1830 hours only to find it abandoned. Of major concern was our fuel situation. The mountainous terrain with its numerous switch-backs had sucked our APCs dry. Even with our foresight, we had loaded every APC with as many extra jerry cans that we could find and carry, we were only able to bring our fuel tanks up to 3/4 full status.

After ensuring security was established, we parked off the side of the road at the designated point and hunkered down for the night to see what tomorrow would bring. At midnight, I was awoken by one of our sentries. A UN Military Observer (UNMO) from Panjevo had arrived to see me. He stated that a staff car would pick me up at 0730 hours the next morning to take me to see Lieutenant-General Morillon at his hotel. At that time, he assured me, I would be briefed on the mission – something I was happy to hear since to date we had only the flimsiest of details.

The following morning I waited for a pick-up that never materialized. Shortly after 0700 hours, 14 Belgian military trucks laden with humanitarian supplies arrived at the rendezvous point. A brief discussion with the Belgian major in charge of the trucks determined that he too had the skimpiest of details concerning the mission. Nonetheless, while we waited we discussed the composition of the convoy and how we would integrate the trucks within the armed escort. One problem became evident immediately. The slow moving (30-40 km / hour) APCs were a terrible match for the 5 ton military trucks that could move at speeds upwards of 80 km / hour. Protection can normally be achieved through armour or speed. Our convoy had neither.

As we worked out some details and SOPs, since this was the first opportunity we had to speak despite the complex nature of the mission, we were deluged by a swarm of reporters who suddenly descended upon us like voracious locusts. They clamoured over our APCs without the slightest hesitation and without seeking permission. All were desperately looking for the best vantage point for pictures. The next act in this poorly choreographed play was not hard to figure out.

Within minutes, at 0745 hours, an avalanche of UN 4x4 Sport Utility Vehicles (SUVs) exploded onto an already surreal scene. The vehicles parked all over – wherever a spot could be found and the UNMO teams poured out of their vehicles. In all the commotion an officer found me and ushered me over to a black staff car that was parked in the middle of the road strangely immune from the high level of aimless activity that now surrounded the convoy. As I approached, a black door was suddenly flung open. As I looked in, Morillon flung out his arm and we shook hands as I stooped in the doorway of his vehicle. He provided no plan or explanation. He merely introduced himself and queried if I was the convoy commander. Once we established that I was, he simply told me that he would meet us at the bridge at 0830 hours and that he was now going to clear our passage. With that he pulled his door shut and the car sped off without warning leaving me standing in the middle of the road inhaling his exhaust fumes.

What followed next was pure bedlam. As the UNMO teams noticed the staff car dart off, they all scrambled for their vehicles. It was a frenzy of sudden activity and amazingly similar to lifting a rock and seeing a multitude of insects scurrying for cover. They then chased off after Morillon leaving our convoy all of a sudden in serene calmness.

The whirlwind of activity disappeared as quickly as it arrived. Yet, in the wake of the meeting with Morillon, it became clear there was no plan and no clear direction. It appeared the press had pegged him correctly. Their assessment in the journals described him as "erratic and indifferent."[3] This impromptu mission, from the start, had the air of an ad hoc spontaneous effort. In fact, the Belgian trucks were originally scheduled for Zepa but were re-routed at the last moment. It quickly appeared as if we were part of an attempt at grand standing – to what end one can only surmise.

I quickly conferred with the Belgian officer in charge of the trucks to pass on to him my rather sketchy direction from Morillon and confirm our order of march for the vehicles. Confusion quickly became evident. I had understood Morillon to mean that we would rendezvous (RV) at the Karakj Bridge at Zvornik only about 20 km down the road. However, the Belgian major insisted Morillon's staff informed him that the RV would be at the Ljobovija Bridge that was very close to Srebrenica itself. This option seemed to make sense – our slower moving convoy could save time by travelling to our destination while Morillon "finalized" our passage. This proved to be another leap of faith that was a very silly assumption.

Our convoy pulled out and drove along the Drina River to our "intended" RV. The scenery was spectacular. We ran into our first forewarning of trouble at Vela Reka. A couple of armed police / militia waved us down in an attempt to stop us. I motioned the lead APC to keep going. I was not about to allow two paramilitaries to interfere with our convoy. However, approximately 15-20 kms further up the road at Uzovnica, they were waiting for us. Two land rovers blocked the road and immediately to their front arrayed in a semi-circle blocking the route were eight military policemen (MPs) with AK-47 assault rifles, body armour and shiny helmets. This time we stopped.

I immediately dismounted and approached the Serb officer in charge. He was clearly shaken and incredibly nervous. He stated we ran the first road-block and must turn back. I responded that we thought they were merely motioning for us to slow down and I then began to stall for time. After all, I expected Morillon to come whistling down the road behind me with the necessary authority in a matter of minutes.

The Serb officer was very agitated and pleaded with me to turn around and he emphasized that we had no authority to be on this road. After approximately 30 minutes of stalling, a UN van carrying the BH

Command "Public Affairs team" (an American captain and a British Senior Non-Commissioned Officer (NCO)) arrived to inform me that "everything went to shit in Zvornik." Furthermore, they stated the convoy was required to return to its start point. It now became clear that Morillon had not already cleared this mission with the host country. It really was an impromptu affair.

With this latest information, I relented and turned the convoy around. On our return trip locals all along the route laughed at us and made universally understood gestures. Once we arrived in Zvornik the same level of chaos became evident. One of Morillon's staff officers told me to jump into his van for a quick ride over to where the negotiations were taking place. Half way across the bridge to the meeting place the van stopped as Morillon's staff car approached. I exited the van to speak to the general when his aide, Major Tucker rolled down the window and yelled out – "we have no authority for the convoy, you wait here and we'll radio you or send an UNMO." He quickly added, "we need an APC as escort" and the car shot away leaving me standing on the bridge looking sorely out of place.

I arrived back at my convoy just in time to see the general's staff car shoot off once again (which reminded me of Tucker's famous line – "the General will not be kept waiting!"). At that point Lieutenant Tom Mykytiuk explained to me that he was told by Major Tucker to provide an APC as an escort. I simply said no – not until we sort out what is going on. At the same time the UNHCR representative, Larry Hollingsworth came over and thanked me for our "initiative" in trying to get through. He then clarified what he thought the plan to be. He mentioned that we had no authority but that Morillon and a small group (i.e. UNHCR representative, 10 ton medical supply truck, 1 APC and 1 UNMO jeep) would go into the pocket and then sort things out. Hot on his heels came a staff officer who at first attempted to order the APC to move-out and, when this failed to get anyone's attention, then succumbed to pleading. He was tasked to organize the escort and since the general had vanished he was beside himself with stress to get going as well.

Now having a better idea of what could laughingly be called a plan, I briefed the designated section commander, as well as his platoon commander of the situation, as well as what I believed his task to be. I also threw in some cheap advice. I then released the APC to join the remainder of the general's entourage so that they could try and catch the shadowy and very elusive BH Commander.

At that point, I had to find a place for our convoy to wait. Serb officials "kindly" guided us to a giant gravel parking lot that was right adjacent to what appeared to be the local dump. This would be home for longer than any of us originally anticipated. Luckily for us, the Belgian transport company called back to their base camp at Panjevo and organized a resupply of 3000 litres of diesel fuel for us. At least one of our worries was solved.

Later in the day we heard that the 10 ton truck had hit a mine on a road going into Srebrenica as it passed through "no-man's land." We found out the next day from our APC (pioneer) Dozer that was allowed access to the site to clear the road, that the route had three feet of snow and the truck swung out from the path that was being used and hit the mine. Luckily, the explosion was totally absorbed by the engine and the Kevlar blankets that lined the cab, thus saving the driver and his partner from any injury.

The following day, 12 March, we had still not heard any news from Morillon in the pocket. Interestingly, a Serb policeman informed us that Serbian television was reporting that General Morillon and the 13 accompanying troops were held captive in Srebrenica by the population who was angry that the UN had done little to help them. Later in the day, we received word through the UNMOs that BH Command in Kiseljak was under the same mindset – Morillon was now a hostage. This was finally confirmed the following day by the Belgian transport company HQ.

Amazingly, the Belgian HQ also attempted to tell us to salvage their 10 ton truck and conduct a reconnaissance to find a new route into Srebrenica as the main bridge was destroyed. Later in the day, our own headquarters relayed a message to us to do the same task. It is always frustrating dealing with HQs that are completely disconnected from where the action is and with staff that has rarely ventured outside of their bunkered operations rooms. We had no freedom of movement. The moment we tried to move roads were blocked. UNMOs that tried to travel in single vehicles were also blocked and even shot at since the belligerents knew they were unarmed. Yet, higher HQs often threw out thoughtless directives as if we were on exercise in a local training area. Fortunately, I was able to report that the truck was non-salvageable and now in a ditch; provide a brief on the condition of the bridge and inform them that the route used was the only available. As always, our pioneers had done their job well! Their after-action report on their recovery effort seemed to anticipate possible queries.[4]

Later that day we also received our first news from the pocket. One of the UNMOs was able to reach the team in Srebrenica by satellite communication (SatCom). He informed us that all were well but he confirmed that they were hostages. He explained that the Muslim population had four conditions for their release: 1. the deployment of a permanent on-site UNMO team; 2. airdrops of humanitarian supplies; 3. authority for the convoy to be allowed through; and 4. a ceasefire.[5] We also learned the Serbs categorically balked at the last two conditions.

On 14 March, day five of the mission, we received word from our BG HQ (relaying orders from BH Command) that we could proceed with the convoy. Happy to see some progress the convoy pulled out of its temporary laager and proceeded up the road. However, 20 km en route progress was halted at Vela Reka by a roadblock. We were immediately informed that we had no authority to proceed. Very quickly Serbian troops began to arrive, as well as a BRDM 2 armoured vehicle that blocked the road and trained its 14.5 mm machine gun on our lead APC.[6] I immediately told the Belgian major to use his SatCom to find out where the authority came from for us to proceed hoping this would clear the impasse. I had to rely on the Belgian communications since we had no equipment that could reach our HQ. Unfortunately, he was required to go through his company HQ, who would then go through battalion HQ, who in turn would contact BH Command. I stalled the Serbs who demanded we turn around hoping that the information that might help us get through would arrive. Our intransigence was beginning to irritate our antagonists. After an hour we finally received a reply from higher HQ. They did not provide us with the information we sought but simply asked us where we were and directed us to return to Zvornik if it was too dangerous or if we were unable to continue.

A journalist later reported to us that local radio stated that the Serbian Ministry of Defence would institute stricter rules for the UN Protection Force (UNPROFOR) because of the "uncooperative behaviour of local UNPROFOR commanders." We constantly received news updates from the bevy of journalists who shadowed our convoy. This was a result of our effort at nurturing a close relationship and providing them with what information we were authorized to reveal. The frank and honest exchange of information (which often meant telling them we could not answer a specific question or provide requested information) paid huge dividends. We received more, as well as more up to date, information that was of use to our mission from them then we did from all of our combined higher HQs put together.

Although difficult to substantiate, I believe that my decision to run the roadblock the first day and my respectful but firm intransigence (when I thought there was something to gain by being uncooperative – i.e. stalling for time) actually earned me the respect of the local commanders. I felt that throughout the entire mission they always dealt with me in a much more respectful and professional manner than they treated others, even those of higher rank.

Another important lesson I later learned was the importance of understanding the limitations of other coalition country participants. In the aftermath of running the roadblock, the Belgian major informed me that his orders from his national command clearly stipulated that at the first sign of danger or potential violence, he was to abandon the mission and return to his base camp. As such, he informed me that in the future the trucks would not continue. Therefore, it made little sense to push the envelope since the whole purpose of the mission was to get the trucks through. No trucks – no need for the escort to carry on alone.

In any case, once again it appeared that we had no authority and would receive none so we returned to our laager at Zvornik. That afternoon, two UNMOs and the UNHCR representative returned from Srebrenica. The head UNMO, a Belgian commandant, was highly emotional and painted a bleak picture. He recounted how Morillon's party had tried to escape twice, once in the APC but the town's people swarmed the vehicle and would not let them move. Apparently, in some cases, mothers actually laid their babies under the tracks of the APC. The second attempt, he explained occurred at night. He stated Morillon was to walk out to an RV where the APC would meet him, however, once again, the moment the APC tried to move it was blocked by a human wall. The Belgian commandant asserted that Morillon "is a hostage." He added, the population threatened to kill all of the UN troops unless the convoy was allowed in.

His description of Srebrenica was equally dismal. He described thousands of refugees living in the streets, with more coming every day. There was no electricity, many wounded and actually no leadership in place. The Belgian officer painted a scene of virtual anarchy. What proved worrisome was his belief that the general was prepared to get himself out at any expense. As useful as it was to finally receive some information of inside the pocket, his briefing was very "doomsdayish" and instilled an attitude of near panic among the UNMO teams. A major issue of concern from the senior UNMOs present seemed to be how to control information, specifically how to feed information to the press without letting any of the real facts out of the bag.

The situation was ridiculous. Trapped in Srebrenica, cut off from his own HQ, and dependent on the Serb authorities to authorize passage of the convoy, Morillon was virtually helpless to solve the problem. Nonetheless, the next morning, 15 March 1993, at 0820 hours we received word from our higher HQs that we now had authority to proceed. However, once again we were stopped at Vela Reka with the same results. It also became evident that more and more troops were being funnelled into the area. The moment we neared the village a large 2 ton truck was driven across the road; the BRDM 2 also arrived and straddled the road and Serbian troops would appear from nowhere and position themselves along the entire convoy. In addition, teams of marksmen with Dragonov sniper rifles suddenly appeared on the roofs of the two story buildings along the road and you could also see soldiers inside the buildings partly hidden by the curtains that were pulled back.

In reaction to the hostile posture we later developed some SOPs and immediate action drills (e.g. use of smoke, covert signals for readying weapons, target designations between vehicles, as well as between individuals inside vehicles, and steps for ensuring vehicles did not bunch/close up even when host country forces insisted you do so "to avoid impeding traffic"). Nonetheless, it became very clear to me at that moment that a major shortcoming in preparation for this convoy was detailed discussions, training and rehearsals of how to fight when in a stopped convoy posture. Moreover, I regretted not bringing grenades for this "humanitarian" mission as they would have been an excellent means of clearing belligerents who were standing guard beside the APCs in the event of a firefight.

Once again, no progress was made and we returned to our laager. However, we did hear from the UNMO net, as well as from the Serbian liaison officer attached to them, that General Ratko Mladic and Lieutenant-General Morillon were to meet that night at the Ljubovija bridge (if he could get out of Srebrenica).

The next day, 16 March, very little changed. The Chief Military Observer (CMO) from BH Comd, a Belgian colonel, arrived to take over negotiations. It now appeared that the Serbs would allow the trucks into the pocket but without the escort. This was unacceptable to everyone, especially the Belgians who were not willing to proceed without protection. The Belgian colonel returned from another meeting and confirmed that Morillon and the others were hostages. He also stated that the general was trying to reach a deal whereby he could be replaced in the pocket by 12 and later went as high as 35 UNMOs so that he could get out. The UNMOs, not surprisingly, did not like the plan.

However, in all fairness, Morillon's effectiveness in the pocket was nil. He had to have freedom of movement to negotiate. The supposed meeting of the previous night between him and Mladic did not happen. It was scheduled for this night as well, but also fell through because the Muslims in Srebrenica would not allow him to leave. At this meeting, I suggested BH Command tell the truth – allow the media to announce that Morillon and other UN troops were being held hostage and allow world opinion to pressure the Muslims to release him. Those present agreed – those at higher HQ vetoed the idea.

What was becoming clear was the mess that this poorly thought out stunt was creating. The commander of BH Command was held hostage and unable to exercise effective command and control. Furthermore, according to our press sources, because of our efforts to get into Srebrenica, the Serbs closed their borders and five UN aid convoys were now blocked.

Despite the gloom there seemed to be a plan in play. There was to be an exchange of "refugees." The plan called for the convoy to go in, deliver supplies and then take out as many Muslims as possible and deliver them to Tuzla, where the trucks would then take on Serbs who were trapped there and bring them back to Serb territory. We all waited for instruction from BH Command who in turn were waiting for direction from their higher HQ in New York. In the end, I was told to be ready to go in the next day. This direction was followed by an array of very pessimistic opinions of what lay in store for us.

Upon return to my "camp" at the dump, I held an orders group to update all crew commanders and to go through our plan for the following day. We made a model of Srebrenica with all the heavy weapon positions, road blocks and obstacles that we were aware of based on the information gathered from the UNMOs who returned from the pocket and our own pioneers. We discussed immediate action drills (e.g. mine strikes, blown tracks, breakdowns), danger areas, specific tasks and arcs of fire. Very quickly it took on the air of an armed raid rather than a humanitarian convoy. In many ways, however, that was the nature of operations in that environment.

The next day opened overcast and cool. Things would not get better. Captain McDon, an UNMO, briefed us that Morillon wanted the convoy to proceed without the escort. McDon also stated that "they are hostages... being guarded so they have to be careful what they say." He also informed us that the pocket was cut in half and the Muslim soldiers were abandoning their uniforms and rifles. Conversely, I was also told by a BBC reporter that ABC had footage showing Morillon addressing crowds in Srebrenica. She felt that "he's turned the situation around and is now in control."

But in the end, our problem was still 'what goes in does not seem to come out.' And the emphasis from BH Command was now to extract our people out of Srebrenica. As such, I asked the Chief UNMO and senior representative from BH Command for clarification on the use of force to get out of the pocket. After all, the implications of what I was told to do could have included the death of innocent civilians if we were to indiscriminately clear a path and force our way out. His reply opened potential ethical dilemmas I hoped I would not have to resolve. "Whatever force required," he reinforced, "in military terms means deadly force." I acknowledged, but asked him to confirm that direction with higher. Those words are easily spoken, particularly by those who do not have to put them into action, but the consequences are always damning.

Further frustration was met in trying to sort out our passage. It appeared that authority was being hammered out due to high level meetings between the UN and the Serbian authorities. I suggested we ensure we have a Serbian liaison officer with us, with the needed communications to talk with their higher HQ so that any impasse could be dealt with quickly and effectively. However, the colonel felt that the presence of UNMOs would be sufficient.[7]

Added to the mix came another nightmare – the arrival of representatives from a Non-Governmental Organization (NGO). The last thing I wanted was to be responsible for civilians who felt they were immune from direction or oversight, but expected protection and rescue when they got in over their heads because of inexperience or arrogance. They would not let me down! They were introduced at a meeting the colonel held that day to bring everybody up to speed on the latest details. The leader of the *Medcins Sans Frontiere* (MSF) team revealed that they were pressured to come by Morillon, who "officially stated the establishment of a headquarters in Srebrenica."[8] The MSF team leader stated they would send only three personnel into the pocket because of the danger and that they would stay only as long as they were safe.

That evening I also received information from my own HQ, which was always very welcome. Because of the distances involved, our available communications equipment and an intervening mountain range, we were able to get High Frequency (HF) communications only sporadically and that usually only in the mornings. However, the innovation of then Master-Corporal Kevin Earl paid great dividends. He was able to build an improvised HF antennae and manipulate it so that he opened a further window of communications between us and BG HQ from 1530 to 1630 hours. This proved useful on a number of occasions.

Day nine, opened overcast and rainy. And it would not improve. At 0730 hours, a new Belgian transport major arrived with new trucks filled with supplies.[9] He passed on to me instructions from BH Command – we were to leave at 0800 hours, arrive at Bratunac at 1100 hours, fix the destroyed bridge, unload the supplies, stay the night and take the refugees out the next morning. Clean and simple! I'm not sure why we did not come up with such a fool proof and logical plan ourselves. Oh yeah, because things are a bit different in real life, on the ground, then they are in a distant HQ. I guess it escaped them that there were some other players involved who might have a say. When I checked with the BH Command colonel on the ground, he had heard nothing.

At noon, however, we received word to go, even though local Serb authorities told us no authority had been given. Nonetheless, our convoy departed under the glare of media cameras. It became quite a circus. A CNN van dodged in and out of the convoy trying to get footage. At one point it cut in front of an APC and slowed right down. Then the rear doors opened up and a cameraman started filming. Their slow speed to allow for filming actually separated the integrity of the convoy.[10]

Once again we were stopped at Vela Reka. However, the Serb posture this time was far more aggressive and strong. The road was blocked by a 2 ton truck, police truck and the BRDM 2. The area swarmed with armed troops and the buildings and roofs were occupied. Of note, was the fact that all soldiers had their weapons at the ready and actually had their fingers on the trigger guards. The soldiers themselves also had a very professional look to them. All appeared well disciplined, had clean, well turned out uniforms, were well groomed and their weapons were similarly immaculate. For this reason, it was a bit of a surprise when a Serb officer reinforced that we required authority to proceed and further warned the colonel that the next time he could not guarantee the safety of the convoy since the "soldiers may fire because they are very nervous." These troops appeared the most professional of any we had yet encountered.

The stand-off had been very tense for both sides. The change in attitude and posture in the Serbs, as well as the increased number of forces dedicated to blocking our passage had been substantial. For that reason, when we received word at 1630 hours that the trapped BH Commander wanted us to force our way through at night seemed ludicrous. We had primitive and very limited numbers of night vision equipment. The road was narrow and ideal country for an ambush. And, at night, in the dark where it is difficult to comprehend what is happening or who instigated an action, a single shot by a nervous, inexperienced or malicious individual could trigger catastrophic consequences. I spoke with both my HQ and the CMO to counsel against such a move. However, word came back that the BH Commander understood "it could get nasty," however, he wanted us to show UN resolve. I was informed that the sense of urgency "in New York" was such that they wanted some form of action to be taken.

I then discussed with the CMO the catch 22 of the Belgian transport company. If we were fired at, in accordance with the rules of engagement

I would return fire and take the necessary action to protect the convoy. However, I had already been informed by the Belgians that if any shots were fired, or if there was an appearance that danger would be imminent they would abort the mission. Therefore, what was the intended objective. He had no clear answer.

We prepared for the mission. I once again gathered the crew commanders together and we discussed immediate action drills and specifically target designation. I explained that all should be alert and closely observe the belligerents. Crews were to focus on targets and determine who would take out who and / or what first, dependent on the threat. Fortuitously, at 1830 hours we were told to ignore the command. There would be no convoy until 0700 hours the next morning.

It was now Day 10 and things seemed to look up. Brigadier-General Pelnasse, the UNPROFOR CMO arrived with a Russian colonel liaison officer to assist in our passage. We also heard that we would get a Serbian military police escort all the way to Bratunac. We departed at 1000 hours after much confusion and contradictory information. However, we were stopped less than five kilometres up the road. But, as always, we held our ground – hoping that something would give. Word started to pass that Lieutenant-General Morillon had actually been allowed out of the pocket and that he was on his way. At 1120 hours he arrived and in a very excited state and started arguing with the Serb police. In a cloud of "*il me bloque*" he disappeared to see the local commander.

He later returned to inform us that we must take the route through Bosnian Serb territory at the Karakaj crossing. As a result, we turned the convoy around and proceeded as instructed. Once we arrived at the crossing site the convoy was again halted. Morillon's vehicle and an UNMO 4x4 were well ahead of the convoy. I was given a motorolla radio so that I could communicate on the UNMO net. Over this means I heard that Morillon had been given clearance to proceed through the barrier. His vehicle and that of an UNMO team shot off without hesitation. I called to inform them to wait and ensure the barrier remained open, as the much slower convoy was just beginning to make the turn towards the crossing point. To no avail. Immediately upon Morillon's staff car and the UNMO jeep clearing the roadblock, the barrier was lowered stopping all other traffic. The BH Command CMO was already there and he was heatedly arguing with the guards and began trying to push them aside. As

I rushed to the barrier, two guards cocked their weapons and fired warning shots into the air. There was suddenly a wild melee of activity as UNMOs, Serbian police and soldiers all rushed around jostling each other.

In the midst of this pandemonium, two of the MSF doctors came rushing to me virtually hysterical that their colleague was being dragged away by Serbian soldiers. I quickly rushed to the scene and ripped him away from the Serbs, passing him to two of my soldiers with instruction to lock up all three MSF medical personnel in our APC ambulance for protection. The Serb soldiers caught initially by surprise quickly regrouped and made an effort to push me aside to retrieve their "prisoner."[11] I physically blocked their passage, gave a loud and aggressive "hey" and pointed at my rank insignia. They scoffed but nonetheless backed-off. I gambled that professional soldiers will always be leery of overstepping their bounds with superior officers. This is a gamble that will not always work. Fortunately, it did this time.

Morillon had returned and the shots, as well as the melee going on seemed to subdue him to a degree. He told the UN personnel to cease all activity and wait for the local brigade commander to arrive. At the same time a local transit bus arrived with reinforcements loaded down with grenades and five RPG-18 anti-tank weapons. After a short while the young Serbian brigade commander, only a major, arrived and authorized passage of the convoy, less the escort. Morillon agreed. This would set a dangerous precedent. I quickly protested, as did the colonel, but the BH Commander simply stated that he was in command and the trucks proceeded alone.
The "B" Coy escort and attachment returned to its laager. Our BG HQ ordered us to stay in the proximity for follow on operations, potentially insertion into the pocket. In addition, there was a plan to use the empty trucks (once unloaded) to transport refugees from Srebrenica to Tuzla. The next seven days became a blurr as negotiations and plans for everything from refugee exchanges to troop rotation in the pocket to troop extraction took place.

While this was going on our troops in the pocket led by Sergeant Gordon Morrison conducted themselves in an exemplary manner. Morillon would later write, "the crew of 42B also performed an outstanding job reducing tension in Srebrenica and reassuring the population with their constant good humour, [and] patrols around the town." This came at a price. On

24 March, Master-Corporal Donald Paris and Private Tim Parrell were wounded during an artillery barrage. Paris suffered a shrapnel wound while Parrell incurred a triple skull facture.[12]

By 31 March, it became apparent that we had done all we could do. Several convoys had evacuated refugees from Srebrenica and the question of inserting troops into the pocket as a deterrent was underway. However, our BG HQ had already decided that if and when, this would happen, a fresh full strength company would take on the task. In the interim, Captain Tom Mykytiuk and his APC crew and a bevy of UNMOs were left in the pocket to establish a UN presence.[13] As such, on Day 22, we were given permission to return to our base camp in Kislejak. We arrived the next day.

On 20 April 1993, Captain Mykytiuk and his crew were relieved in place by "G" Coy, 2 RCR BG. An agreement had been reached between the UN and the Serbian government to make Srebrenica a UN Protected Area. As a result, "G" Coy was authorized passage into the enclave to begin demilitarizing the pocket.[14]

LESSONS REINFORCED

I will not be so bold or naïve as to attempt to list "lessons learned" as what I have to share based on this experience are lessons that are not unique but timeless themes that must be reinforced and remembered when on operations. First, always plan for the worst possible case – anything else then becomes gravy. Part of this entails rehearsals. If you have the time rehearse every possible contingency. If time is short, at least do a chalk talk, or discussion on possible scenarios so you and your subordinate leaders can talk through possible actions. Encourage your subordinates to do the same with their troops. Although we had SOPs and immediate action drills, and had practiced convoy operations in both Canada and Croatia, it was not until we faced our first confrontation that I actually realized we had never rehearsed close combat drills from a stopped APC at a road block in detail. As a result we had to develop specific contingency plans during the mission.

The second point is always promote an attitude of self-sufficiency, innovation and adaptability. The reason we were able to cope with a "short duration mission" that lasted 22 days was due to the fact that from the beginning we packed our APCs for every possible contingency and we briefed all to conserve absolutely everything right from the start. In fact, Morillon would later write, "the comprehensive and farsighted way in which they and their vehicle had been equipped enabled us to cope with the extraordinary situation in Srebrenica."[15]

A third point to be reinforced is always ensure you have the fullest possible understanding of those you are working with and against. This is even more important in the new integrated paradigm. For instance, it is critical to know the commander's intent (and the underlying motives that drive it, whether they be rooted in guidance from the UN, the coalition HQ, a specific nationality, particularly the commander's own national command, or personal). The spectre of "national command" direction is huge, particularly in UN missions. If a component of your team has specific national command direction, it could completely alter how you go about your mission. For example, the Belgian direction to avoid any confrontation or danger – immediately negates certain actions on the part of the escort. Conversely, if the mission is driven by motives not in consonance with your own national command intent or approval, your potential actions will also be potentially constrained. In the end, ensure you have the confidence and courage to do the right thing. Do not necessarily assume that foreign commanders in a UN or coalition setting will task you in the best interest of your nation or men.

Similarly, understand the other organizations you are working with. Get to know the individuals, their motives for being there, their operating pro-cedures, their expectations and their capabilities. If civilians, whether UN or NGO, accompany you, ensure you assign an escort to them responsible for keeping an eye on them, particularly during times of crisis or chaos. Although this may seem like a burden, it could save you a lot of trouble in the end. However, it should always be remembered that these individuals are often very experienced and may have a lot to offer to you as well.

In regard to the press, always remember that they have a job to do as well and attempt to provide them as much information as you possibly can in accordance with regulations. By cooperating, you provide a better chance that they get the story right. It also allows an opportunity to showcase what the nation, and particularly CF service personnel are achieving. Furthermore, the press is often a great source of information. Normally, if you treat them with respect and courtesy, they return the favour.

The fourth point is to maintain a professional demeanour at all times regardless of how your adversary behaves. The conduct and professionalism of you and your troops can have a dramatic impact on situations. Confidence, competency and effectiveness normally resonate with professional behaviour. As such, opponents are less likely to try to push the envelope if they feel they are up against a professional force to be reckoned with. Moreover, often times it breeds reciprocal behaviour. The mission in question demonstrated that. Throughout our epic saga, despite several tense stand-offs, the Serbian leadership and troops were always respectful to my soldiers and me as we were to them. When it was time to finally leave the area, we were allowed to pass the famous Karakj Bridge at Zvornik, which was often a feat of its own, with no hassles. Conversely, during our stay another Canadian convoy arrived, returning from Macedonia and tried to get across the bridge. They stopped approximately 200 metres from the structure, their vehicles parked haphazardly on the road, blocking local traffic. The officer in charge, flak vest wide open, helmet without the chin strap done up, got out, planted himself in the middle of the road and pulled out his binoculars to "recce" the bridge, while his C-9 gunner adopted what he thought was an imposing intimidating stance beside him. The unnecessarily belligerent and unprofessional posture was ridiculous, particularly in the semi-residential area. I quickly approached the officer in charge and shared my observations with him, however, I suspect the damage had already been done. They never got across the bridge and had to take an alternate route that added days to their journey.

The fifth and final "lesson" I will reinforce is always maintain sanitary conditions and ensure personal hygiene is being practiced. Although this seems like motherhood I am always amazed at how many individuals do not do it. For instance, no one imagined we would be in the laager for three weeks. However, the first day we established, as per normal army practice, a "pissing point" and set up a toilet (portable seat and plastic bag) in the field away from our vehicles to minimize contamination of our living area. We briefed the entire convoy, but amazingly, I had to get the NCOs to police the actual laager because initially the Belgian and French troops attached to us would get out of their trucks and try to urinate beside their vehicles, in lanes that were only about a metre wide and through which people would walk. In addition, ensuring individuals washed and shaved daily, not only provided routine, which in itself often lessens stress, but it also helped in keeping levels of sickness down.

Keeping in mind that you are on your own, and never sure for how long, it is important to ensure the well being of your personnel. As such, hygiene, which is often neglected, is a key factor. Historically, disease and sickness have always claimed more casualties than combat.

As stated, these lessons are not necessarily unique or new. However, they are worth reinforcing. As a closing note, I realize there is one last point to make – trust your soldiers and make good use of their ideas and strengths. It has never failed to amaze me how professional and effective they are. In the case of this mission, where success was achieved, it was a direct result of their efforts. Given the chance to perform they will never let you down.

ENDNOTES

1   The "B" Coy element of the convoy consisted of 5 M113 Armoured Personnel Carriers (APCs), 1 APC Pioneer (pioneer) Dozer, 1 APC MRT (Maintenance, Repair, Technical vehicle), 1 APC Ambulance and three French engineer vehicles – snow plough, snow blower, cargo truck).

2   The details of this chapter are based on entries from my personal diary. Quotations from other people are also taken from this diary unless otherwise accredited.

3   James Graff, "Hell in a Small Place," *Time*, 29 March 1993, 27.

4   Amazingly, the Serbs had allowed the single APC (pioneer dozer) access to the wreckage. Apparently, they too wanted the road cleared.

5   At 1500 hours we were told by a reporter from Reuters that Sarajevo radio will have a message from Morillon later in the day stating he is in Srebrenica of his own free will.

6   I was actually busy trying to negotiate / stall for time and had not noticed the MG being trained on our vehicles. Then Master-Corporal (now Lieutenant) Kevin Earl immediately brought it to my attention. He was concerned that a negligent discharge could start a firefight with serious consequences for all. I spoke to the Serb officer commanding what was obviously their rapid reaction unit and shared our concerns. He immediately ordered the BRDM gunner to elevate the MG. Throughout the mission I was blessed with a fantastic HQ crew – then Master-Corporal Earl and Corporals Cane and Farrow. Their initiative, coolness under pressure and courage made my job so much easier. I regret never fully telling them how much I appreciated their assistance and presence.

7   Sergeant Vale, a British NCO who was attached to the mission by BH Command as a public relations representative observed that UNMO seemed to stand for "U"nable to "N"egotiate, "M"ove or "O"rganize.

8   It is still unclear where this direction came from as he was ostensibly incommunicado. It could have been through the UNMOs. Furthermore, the team leader stated other NGOs were also pressured to send representatives. None did.

9   After two days in the laager the Belgians decided to return to their base camp in Panchevo, which was approximately two hours away. Whenever, word came for the convoy to proceed they duly arrived and when we were thwarted returned to their base camp.

10   When I attempted to chastise the CNN reporter later in the day, he merely blew me off. He stated security of the convoy was my responsibility and getting the story was his. Despite this incident and the overwhelming arrogance of the CNN crew, relations with the other press outlets and reporters were first rate. Most were exceptionally considerate and professional.

11   The MSF doctor in question had dismounted from the UNHCR truck he had been traveling in and began taking pictures during the melee. The Serbs grabbed him and his camera. After the crisis had subsided I was able to retrieve his camera less the film. All three MSF doctors chose not to go through to Srebrenica with aid trucks as a result of the experience. However, the doctor who was snapped by the Serbs and rescued, later had a rush of bravado and complained to the CMO that I had stopped him against his will from going into Srebrenica. The surgeon of the group later cleared the air and stated that this was not the case. In fairness to the MSF team, the team leader later came to me and apologized as well.

12   Both were evacuated by helicopter and recovered from their wounds. The other members of the section were Daniel McAllister and Private Charron. They were later replaced by Captain Tom Mykytiuk and his crew that included Master-Corporal Tate, Corporals Postma, Zalik, Mayo and Private Bush. Like the troops before them, they distinguished themselves through their courage and humanity. During a severe artillery barrage, they risked their own lives to rescue and evacuate wounded civilians.

13   In regard to the APC and crew left in the pocket, the BG HQ stated, "while not directly tasked with a mission, their presence may be the initial step in creating another UNPA within the Former Republic of Yugoslavia. "Op Instruction – Srebrenica Deployment," 2 RCR Operations Files, 052145 Apr 93.

14   Their tasks included: establishing an Observation Post line to monitor the ceasefire; corralling of weapons; establishing holding areas for non-combatants; security of non-combatants; security of landing zones for medical evacuation operations; and assisting UNHCR in their evacuation of Srebrenica. "Frag O to Srebrenica Deployment," 2 RCR Operations Files, 181000 Apr 93. The task was eventually passed to a Dutch battalion. On 11 July 1995, a Serbian offensive captured the safe area and between 6-16 July they expelled 23,000 Bosnian Muslim women and children and captured and executed thousands of Muslim men. See Jan Willem Honig and Norbert Both, *Srebrenica. Record of a War Crime* (London: Penguin Books, 1996), xix.

15   Letter UNPROFOR BH COMD, BHCS/8439, Morillon to Admiral Anderson, CDS, 30 March 1993.

CHAPTER 3

FRONTLINE COMMANDERS: LEADERSHIP CHALLENGES AT THE COMPANY LEVEL IN UNPROFOR 1992/1993

Major Tony Balasevicius

In the late 1990s, the Canadian Forces Officer Professional Development 2020 project concluded that "the Canadian Forces are going through a number of revolutions that taken together will pose significant challenges for leaders in the future."[1] Specifically, their research indicated that future leaders will have to confront a plethora of issues including dealing with the media; being knowledgeable about individual rights and freedoms; having the ability to operate within a technological and information rich environment; and being able to function within complex peacekeeping/peacemaking operations.[2]

For Army leaders who have served on peacekeeping and peacemaking operations during that time, many of these conclusions are little more than formal recognition of a situation that has existed for almost a decade. During that period, successful frontline commanders had to evolve their leadership style to meet the challenges of extremely complex and ambiguous missions. Moreover, they had to do so without the benefit of institutional training or the intellectual development that today's military leaders receive.

Although today's leaders are much better prepared to face the uncertainties of modern conflict than their predecessors, no amount of preparation will cover every possible eventuality that soldiers and their commanders will face in the dynamic that is human conflict. It is therefore important for leaders to be able to recognize and quickly adapt to changing and unfamiliar situations as a matter of routine. This is precisely what Kilo Company, the Second Battalion, The Royal Canadian Regiment (2 RCR) had to do during its deployment into the former Yugoslavia in the fall of 1992.

This chapter will evaluate some of the lessons learned by the company as it attempted to adapt to the demands of modern peacemaking in the Post Cold War era. Specifically, it will look at the actions taken by commanders as they attempted to find solutions to a myriad of issues in an environment where ambiguous mandates and inadequate Rules of Engagement (ROEs) added complexity and uncertainty to the already volatile situation that was the former Yugoslavia in the early 1990s.

International interest in the former Yugoslavia began in June 1991, after Slovenia declared independence from Yugoslavia and conflict erupted with the Serb backed Yugoslav People's Army (JNA). There was little the JNA could do to hold on to the break away republic and, by September, they had started to redeploy their forces. The situation in the region was complicated when Croatia declared independence later in the year. However, unlike Slovenia, which had a homogeneous population, Croatia had areas with substantial Serb minorities and when the declaration was made the JNA moved in to secure Serb interests.[3]

The Security Council responded to the JNA actions by authorizing the deployment of the United Nations Protection Force (UNPROFOR)[4] into areas where the Serbs constituted the majority or a substantial minority. These areas were designated United Nations Protected Areas (UNPA). The arrival of UN peacekeepers into the UNPAs played an important role in securing confidence and the withdrawal of the JNA from Croatia and opened the door for humanitarian agencies to start carrying out their work.[5] Unfortunately, just as the situation in Croatia was beginning to stabilize, fighting erupted to the south in the new Republic of Bosnia-Herzegovina.

Bosnia-Herzegovina (BH) was ethnically heterogeneous and it was unlikely that there would be clear delimitations between areas that wanted to secede and those that did not. In order to find a democratic solution to the problem, the Bosnian government held a referendum on independence. Unfortunately, the Bosnian Serbs, who represented the minority, boycotted the process. Not surprisingly, with the majority of eligible voters voting for independence, the Bosniak[6] and Croat representatives in Bosnia's parliament declared the republic's independence on 5 April 1992. The Serb delegates walked out of the process and declared their own state known as the "Republika Srpska" on midnight 6 April 1992.[7]

When fighting broke out in Bosnia-Herzegovina, the new Republika Srpska had a significant military advantage as they posessed almost all of the heavy weapons in the region. This advantage allowed them to quickly establish control over most of the Serb-populated regions. They were unable, however, to extend their influence into the larger cities such as Mostar and Sarajevo.

Although, much of Sarajevo was controlled by the Bosniaks, the Bosnian Serb Army was able to encircle the city and then impose a blockade upon it. In an effort to establish some stability in the region, the United Nations extended the existing UNPROFOR mandate, which had originally been limited to the deployment of forces into Croatia, to include Bosnia-Herzegovina.[8] Initially, this new mandate was limited to the protection of the Sarajevo International Airport but, as time went on, it was slowly expanded to include the protection of humanitarian aid, assistance in the delivery of relief throughout BH, and to the protection of civilian refugees.[9]

The protection of humanitarian aid and civilian refugees was not the mission of 2 RCR in the summer and early fall of 1992. The unit had just returned to its garrison in Gagetown from a successful peacekeeping tour on the island of Cyprus and had used most of the summer to take leave, complete its annual posting cycle, and provide support to the various courses that were being run at the Army's Combat Training Center (CTC).

By early September, the unit had finished its posting cycle and CTC tasking, and was making final preparations for upcoming Trade Qualification Level 4 (QL 4)[10] courses when speculation began to circulate that the unit might be tasked to assist in UNPROFOR's expanded role in BH. Rumors were confirmed around 20 September 1992, when the unit received orders for its second operational deployment within a year.

The initial plan had called for the 2 RCR Battalion Group (BG) to deploy to Croatia by the end of October 1992, and then move into the area of Banja Luka where it was to start carrying out humanitarian relief operations. Unfortunately, there was significant Bosnian Serb resistance to the idea, which was compounded by a lack of UN commitment to press the issue. This deadlock forced the BG to take up residence in the town of Lipic, Croatia, where it remained for almost three months.

ADJUSTING TO THE NEW REALITIES OF PEACEMAKING IN THE POST COLD WAR WORLD

The BG used its time in Lipic to run badly needed QL 4 courses that were put on hold prior to the unit's deployment. Support was also provided to ongoing operations in the various UNPAs and in early January 1993, Hotel Company with the unit's Reconnaissance Platoon were deployed into the former Yugoslav Republic of Macedonia to monitor developments along the border areas. In mid February 1993, UNPROFOR, with Canadian Government concurrence, ordered the remainder of the BG into the area of Sarajevo to start humanitarian aid operations. Once deployed into BH, the unit was housed in the town of Visoko with two companies, Bravo and Kilo, locating 30 kilometers to the west in the town of Kiseljak.[11]

Kilo Company set up residence in an abandoned brick factory on the outskirts of Kiseljak and within hours of hitting the ground, it was told to be ready to start operations the following day. Over the next few weeks, the company took on an increasing number of diverse missions that included convoy escort, traffic control and security operations, VIP escort, route reconnaissance, and security to infrastructure repair missions.[12] These missions, combined with the normal camp administrative and security tasks, which in themselves required almost 20 percent of the company's resources, placed a great deal of pressure on the company. And it never let up. Adding to these difficulties was the fact that the company was simultaneously undergoing a steep learning curve in a number of different areas.

In an effort to overcome the learning curve and to deal with the sheer number and variety of missions in a systematic way, officers and Senior Non-Commission Officers (NCO) were brought together for brainstorming sessions where various options for each task could be placed on the table and discussed in some detail. These sessions had two benefits; the mission commander would then use the best ideas to develop his concept of operations (COP), and key players became knowledgeable about the various tasks. Although, this process worked well to get things started, the plans often required continuous amendment as the situation on the ground was extremely fluid. In order to keep everyone in the company abreast of the most up to date experiences, time was set aside at the end of each daily conference to talk about what had occurred during the previous 24 hours. Specifically, we reviewed what had worked, and most importantly, what, if anything had gone wrong.

The first officer in the company to debrief an operational experience was Captain Stutt, the mortar platoon commander and the first officer in the company to lead a convoy into Sarajevo. In the summer of 1992, Captain Stutt had been the mortar Subject Matter Expert (SME) at the Army's Infantry School and when 2 RCR received word that it would be deploying to the former Yugoslavia, it was decided that he should be brought to the unit for the mission. This would prove to be a fortuitous decision as Stutt's cool demeanour in high stress situations likely saved the lives of more than a few soldiers. Captain Stutt was given 30 minutes to brief on the convoy mission, followed by a question period.

He started the briefing with a detailed overview of the operation and then went on to discuss the good points, linking everything he said to the original brainstorming session that had occurred the previous day. He then went on to talk about important issues regarding coordination between the military and Non-Governmental Organizations (NGOs) and most importantly, the mistakes that had been made, and the weaknesses with some of the arrangements. The question and answer period that followed lasted almost an hour.

The major point that was brought forward during this briefing was that both sides (military and NGO) had arrived at the rendezvous (RV) point on the first day uncertain about how to coordinate their efforts.[13] An initial period was needed to establish a relationship, and this proved critical to developing Standard Operating Procedures (SOPs) that both sides could work with. Stutt indicated that he focused his initial efforts with the NGOs on explaining the military's method of operation, more specifically, its capabilities and limitations. After some trial and error, eventually both sides were able to work together relatively effectively. This first debriefing session proved so successful that the after-action briefing became an important part of the company's SOPs.

The passing on of experience and knowledge became an important element in the company's ability to adjust to new situations and it was not confined to the company level or simply when taking on new missions. Over time, policies were instituted whereby no standing task was to be undertaken without half the organization involved having completed the task at least once before. This policy could not always be followed, but leaders in the company understood the benefits and strived to minimize occasions when it could not be followed. In order to provide the BG with the benefit of the Company's experience, SOPs also directed that a "Lesson Learned" paragraph be included in all routine reports being sent up the chain of command.

The key lessons that came to the forefront during the company's initial deployment into Bosnia-Herzegovina and the startup of operational taskings focused on the leadership's ability to adapt to new and quickly changing circumstances. The methods needed to keep the organization on top of any given situation revolved around a focus on detailed planning and the leveraging of experience from throughout the organization rather than from a few key individuals.

As peacekeeping/peacemaking operations became more complex and decentralized, it became clear that company leaders were no longer able to carry all of the technical skills and knowledge necessary to complete the tasks assigned. It became clear that to achieve success in the new environment, leadership styles had to evolve to a more team-orientated participative approach where team members brought specific skill, knowledge and experience that was shared and blended together to achieve team goals. During the initial deployment and subsequent operations in Bosnia-Herzegovina, the key to Kilo Company's success in dealing with the constant changes and ambiguity was the power of experience and the continuous and timely exchange of information with the people who needed it the most. That operational information was exchanged through such venues as routine reports, brainstorming sessions and after-action briefings.

Brainstorming sessions bring the resources and experience of the company to the mission commander. They can be used at any time during the planning process, but need to be structured so that they do not devolve into a free for all. They are most important during the early stages of a deployment, but should be used whenever a new situation arises or when commanders are unfamiliar with the task they are to undertake. Brainstorming sessions work well when combined with the after-action briefing as a way to move information and lessons learned within an organization in a structured way.

Like brainstorming sessions, after-action briefings are extremely important during first time missions or when mistakes have occurred. The after-action briefing must focus on identifying and fixing the problem not fixing blame! As a general guideline, everyone must first agree on what happened. Once this has been established, the person organizing the event needs to concentrate on what went well (10 percent), what needs to change (90 percent) and then spend as much time as is necessary ensuring everyone understands the lessons that came out of the process. The key to making this system work was to convince everyone in the company that they would be helping the organization and not providing the chain of command with quality rope with which to hang the company. Now that the Canadian Army uses the after-action review process as an SOP for training, it should be a natural event to carry this process over to operations.

The use of brainstorming sessions and after-action reviews are not just a good training tool. When used during operations in BH, they increased understanding, trust and cohesion within the company. More importantly, the company found that it eliminated uncertainty both within the leadership and in the ranks, which tended to reduce stress by makng soldiers confident that their leadership was on top of issues that had a direct impact on them. Another important lesson that came out of the experience was that the most underutilized resource in the Army is the senior NCO corps. During brainstorming sessions and after action reviews, their input was invaluable in solving many of the operational problems and more importantly, the collaboration issues between the military and civilian.

Collaboration between military and civilian organizations is a subject that needs to be addressed in some detail. If the military and other national and international organizations are going to continue to work together, some type of prior training or, at the very least familiarization, is needed for both communities. Training needs to include basic operating practices such as policies at checkpoints, communications while en route, pre-inspections, etc. The integration of such training during the early phases of deployment would significantly reduce the initial period of confusion as each new organizational mix attempts to develop SOPs to meet local conditions.

Finally, military organizations undertaking humanitarian assistance missions must be flexible and anticipate the fact that they will end up doing far more then they initially expected. For example, the protection of humanitarian assistance can included a wide range of additional tasks such as: security for convoys and warehouses, the protection of refugees and safe zones, disarmament of combatants and security of demilitarization areas, and providing security to headquarters and support organizations that are within the area of operations. More importantly, each of these tasks needs different sets of capabilities that may or may not be available to the commander on the ground. Regardless of the organizational makeup for the specific task the fundamental rule that must never be compromised is that any task must be capable of providing a big bang for the buck if it has to fight.

REALITY CHECK:
THIS IS NOT YOUR NORMAL PEACEKEEPING MISSION

In early March 1993, fighting intensified in eastern Bosnia-Herzegovina[14] as Bosnian Serb paramilitary units launched a general offensive along the Drina valley, attacking several cities including Srebrenica. These attacks resulted in a heavy loss of life among the civilian population and severely impeded United Nations humanitarian efforts in the area.[15]

As the UN was attempting to find a solution to the Serb aggression and reestablish humanitarian relief in the area, Kilo Company had moved beyond its initial learning curve and appeared to be adjusting to the operational situation around Kiseljak and Sarajevo. Unfortunately, the confidence gained during the preceding weeks was to be shattered on 25 March 1993, as the events of that day were to provide the company leadership with a far more complex dimension of direct command and one for which the company was not prepared.

At 0711 hours (hrs), on 25 March 1993, Captain Toma, the mortar platoon second-in-command, joined the company net indicating he was departing camp to pick up a UN High Commission for Refugee (UNHCR) convoy located just outside Kiseljak.[16] Captain Toma was one of the youngest and hardest working officers in the company. He was also an excellent writer with an ability to quickly dissect complex situations, a combination that made him an ideal candidate to become the first company operations officer. For this mission, he was in call sign (C/S) 51B, and had 52C, 52D, 61E, and 53D under his command.

At 0810 hours, Toma's escort picked up the convoy at the RV and headed into Sarajevo.[17] The convoy arrived at the Sarajevo International Airport sometime around 0903 hrs and, after a brief stay, moved on to the PPT building where the UNHCR trucks began unloading supplies for local distribution.[18] By 0950 hrs, Toma's escort had moved back to the airport to wait for the trucks and the return trip to Kiseljak.[19]

Shortly after the escort arrived at the airport, the UNHCR representative called to state that the road from the PPT building to the Airport had been closed and that the aid trucks would spend the night at the PPT building. Toma decided to return the escort to Kiseljak and, following company SOPs, lead the advance guard of three APS out of the city. As Toma passed the final Serb checkpoint leading out of Sarajevo fighting broke out within the inner city, closing all roads. The situation forced Warrant Officer Blair Parks, who was in command the remaining APCs, to remain in place at the Airport.[20] At around 1200 hrs, the escort prepared to eat lunch in the back of the carriers, which was to prove fortunate because at around 1230 hrs, six to eight rounds of mortar fire landed in the location of the sitting vehicles.[21] Although, no injuries were sustained, there was significant splash (hits) on most of the vehicles.

Corporal Woods' vehicle, 52D received 23 hits, while Private McCormick's vehicle C/S 51B received a total of 26 hits, and Private Sparks' vehicle C/S 61E had an incredible 70 hits. After the attack Warrant Officer Parks quickly ordered all vehicles secured and moved the convoy's personnel into the airport's bunkers, where they remained until about 1443 hrs, when word was passed down that the fighting had stopped and that the escort was authorized to depart the city.[22] Although, a number of individual soldiers within the company had received close calls prior to this event, Toma's escort was the first time there had been a real possibility of large numbers of company soldiers being killed.

Needless to say, there was great joy in the Canadian camp when the convoy returned safely home. Unfortunately, the euphoria of getting everyone out of Sarajevo alive was short lived. At 1700 hrs, C/S 55B and 55D (members of the anti-armour platoon) had finished their traffic control and security task along the Tarcin-Kresovo road.[23] As 55B was returning to camp, the M-113 armoured personnel carrier (APC) attempted to give an oncoming car some room and moved onto the shoulder of the road, regrettably, the shoulder gave way forcing the vehicle down the embankment and causing it to overturn. Although the crewmembers in the turret were physically okay, the driver was killed. Over the next few days, it became increasingly clear that these two events were having a significant and negative impact on the company and something needed to be done. The question was what?

Luckily, the Padre had arrived in the camp for critical incident debriefings (CID) and he was asked to provide recommendations on how the company could deal with this situation and, more importantly, how similar events could be handled in the future. The Padre indicated that professional help was an important element in the overcoming of problems related to critical incidents or Post Traumatic Stress Disorder (PTSD) but that, in many cases, the first point of contact for aid was usually friends. He went on to explain that soldiers could be affected by a specific event if it was traumatic enough or by an accumulation of smaller events. He also stated that it was difficult to predict individual responses. To deal with this issue in a systematic way he recommended that the company set up a "soldier watch system" and that soldiers be encouraged to come forward if they felt a friend was not acting like his or her usual self as they were often the first to notice if things were different with someone close.

With this in mind, the company initiated a brainstorming session where the idea was put to the leadership. The meeting started off by acknowledging that the company was moving into a new phase of the deployment where critical incidents were likely to become more common and that a plan was needed to deal with the situation. The idea of a watch system was brought out and was very well received. During the next hour, the details of how the watch system was to work were ironed out. Soldiers were encouraged to come forward if they felt a friend was not acting in their usual way. Similarly, if leaders noticed a change in a soldier's disposition they were to keep the chain of command informed but were to ask a fellow soldier to have a talk with the individual as a first step. Based on the outcome, the soldier would either be allowed to continue their duties, given light duties around camp, or sent to the medical officer or Padre for further diagnosis.

Another of the Padre's ideas that was adopted was having the company hold an incident debriefing process where soldiers were encouraged to talk about specific events as a group. The main objective of these incident debriefings was to encourage the healing process by opening up unpleasant or painful memories. This was accomplished by having leaders and soldiers talk through the event under the guidance of the Padre. Although there were some initial concerns about the touchy feely aspects of this process, the idea worked extremely well, and the mental and physical state of the company remained extremely strong despite the heavy mission load.

The ultimate weapon on the battlefield is a thinking soldier who has a weapon in his hands and is well trained in its use. It is therefore extremely important that the chain of command be aware of the mental and physical state of this ultimate weapon and monitor any decline in its performance. The watch system is critical to units that are operating in decentralized and complex situations and who do not have the necessary resources at hand. However, once an incident has taken place, some form of incident debriefing process with professional counselors is extremely important.

In many regards, this process is similar to the after-action review as both attempt to detail the specifics about what has happened. Incident debriefings must actively encourage participants to share their emotional responses to the event. According to professor Todd Helmus, the best treatment for soldiers that are suffering from PTS can be "characterized by the acronym PIES: proximity (treat soldier close to the front), immediacy (treat soon after symptom onset), expectancy (reassure that soldier is not ill and that he will return to duty), and simplicity (ensure that soldier has food and drink, and bring body temperature to a normalized state)."[24] Helmus explained that while these "terms illustrate treatment by combat stress control units, they also apply to treatment within the operating unit (provided the tactical situation permits)."[25]

CID should be a routine occurrence following any difficult or especially traumatic event. Special attention must be paid to individuals who show signs of distress during the process and additional follow up may be necessary through personal conversations with friends. The unit Padre is a good candidate to guide the debriefings and any individual follow up that may be needed. It is important to remember that the success of any type of watch / CID system is based on the use of professionals and in convincing the soldiers that their coming forward will not condemn their friends to early release.

STANDOFF AT CHECK POINT S-1

In mid-April 1993, fighting was still ongoing in eastern Bosnia-Herzegovina as Bosnian Serb units were continuing their attack on

Srebrenica. On 16 April, the Security Council, acting under Chapter VII of the Charter, adopted resolution 819 (1993), demanding that Srebrenica be treated as a "safe area." It also called for the immediate withdrawal of paramilitary units from the area and the cessation of attacks against that town. The Council requested that the Secretary-General take steps to increase the presence of UNPROFOR in Srebrenica, and on 21 April, UNPROFOR's Commander reported that 170 UNPROFOR troops, civilian police and military observers had been deployed into Srebrenica and that they had successfully demilitarized the town.[26]

However, most events in BH were connected.   By 21 April 1993, K Company was firmly established in Camp Paardeberg in Kiseljak. Most of the initial construction of camp defences had been completed, and there was a regular rotation of tasks between platoons within the company. Reconnaissance platoon had returned from a successful mission in Macedonia, and was carrying out patrols in the area of Busovaca, while anti-amour platoon commanded by Captain Keith Laughton had been given the very dangerous task of providing security to infrastructure repair missions in downtown Sarajevo. Captain Laughton was one of the more experienced, and by far the most knowledgeable, of the officers in the company. He had been posted from the Army's Director of Land Requirements into the unit the previous summer to command anti-amour platoon.[27] During the course of the deployment, his experience and technical knowledge played an important role in finding solutions to the many issues that came up during the company's brainstorming sessions. On 24 April 1993, Captain Laughton put his experience and knowledge to good use when he became one of the players in the incident that would test the organizational ability and resolve of key company leaders.

On that day, the company was programmed to perform a large number of tasks. Captain Laughton (C/55) was tasked to escort an infrastructure repair mission into Sarajevo to clean sewer pipes; C/S 6 (reconnaissance platoon) was scheduled to carry out two patrols in the area of Busovaca, as well as provide an escort for UNMOs into Zenica. In addition, the company was given a late task to provide six APCs to transport personnel from BH Command to the airport in Sarajevo.[28]   The only saving grace that morning was that mortar platoon (C/S 51), which was scheduled to take a UNHCR convoy into Sarajevo, had their task cancelled at 0847 hrs. Still, the number and types of taskings the company had to undertake on the 24th meant that there would be a significant amount of company activity on the road between Kiseljak and Sarajevo that day.

Activity started at 0700 hrs, when the infrastructure repair mission commanded by Captain Laughton departed camp with three APCs (one of which was a TUA - TOW[29] *Under Armour*). They arrived at checkpoint S-1 at about 0725 hrs and were allowed to pass through after a short delay. Checkpoint S-1 was located on the main route between Kiseljak and Sarajevo just south of Rakovica. The checkpoint was positioned at the end of a long and heavily wooded defile that cut through the side of a hill, making any attempt at maneuvering vehicles extremely difficult. As Captain Laughton departed the checkpoint, he reported that that a T-54/55 tank was at the position and had its gun sighted on the Dutch contingent's shuttle vehicle.[30] Once Laughton had passed the checkpoint, he went on to meet with Captain Rokita, the BH Command liaison officer, and then proceded on to the work site.

Back in Kiseljak, the UNHCR task that had been cancelled earlier in the day was reactivated when UNHCR representatives called at 1410 hrs to ask why the escort was not at the RV point. About 20 minutes later, after a flurry of activity, five APCs commanded by Captain Stutt (C/S 51) pulled out of the camp.[31] Shortly before 1540 hrs, Stutt contacted the company command post to indicate that a Dutch VIP escort returning from Sarajevo Airport was being blamed for using a video camera, which was making it difficult for other traffic to get through S-1.[32] Stutt estimated that it was going to take at least an hour to get the convoy and escort past the checkpoint.[33]

As Serb authorities were searching the UNHCR trucks in C/S 51's convoy, the Dutch VIP escort from Sarajevo arrived at precisely the same time that C/S 52, who was transporting BH Command personnel to the airport, pulled up and tried to get past on a priority clearance. Adding to this confusion was the fact that the Serbs searching the UNHCR vehicles being escorted by Stutt found cargo that had not been manifested.

These events clearly overwhelmed the Serbs and one of the border guards cocked his AK-47 assault rifle; pointing the barrel in the direction of the VIP escort, while the 14.5mm machine gun (MG) on the tank also turned onto the escort. More ominously, the Serbs quickly manned an RPK MG that was located on the second floor of the building being used to support Serb operations at the checkpoint.

At 1610 hrs, C/S 51 reported that some of the UNHCR trucks in the convoy did not have their paperwork properly filled out and that it was going to take some time to get though the checkpoint. Shortly thereafter, the Serbs announced that the vehicle carrying the unregistered goods was to be confiscated. In an effort to reduce tensions, the UNHCR representative explained that the supplies would be taken back to Kiseljak until the proper paper work could be produced and this appeared to be unacceptable to the Serbs who insisted that the goods on the truck now belonged to them. The situation quickly escalated when the UNHCR representative declared that he would rather destroy the merchandise then allow it to be confiscated. At this point Captain Stutt ordered the escort to have all weapons readied.[34]

As the situation continued to deteriorate, the border police called in local military forces and they also insisted that the items carried by the UNHCR were now the property of the Serb authority. As the Serbs attempted to start unloading the items Captain Stutt ordered his men to intervene. Tensions that were already running high became much worse. In fact, at one point, the Serb commander asked Captain Stutt if he was trying to "get me (serb commander) to take you (Stutt) out."[35]

At about 1615 hrs, Captain Stutt radioed in a situation report (SITREP). The confident veteran of over 50 successful escort missions into Sarajevo was clearly concerned with the situation at hand. He indicated that there was a real possibility of a fight and was especially concerned about the tank. He was told that C/S 55 was still in Sarajevo and that the TUA would be recalled to S-1 and positioned to support him. Stutt was also told that once the TOW was in position he had authority to open fire if he felt it was necessary. What was left of the company in camp was brought together as a reserve and moved to an "S" bend (about 600 meters away from the checkpoint). The company command post was then told to inform BG Headquarters of the situation and to ask if the UN ready reserve could be activated.[36]

At about 1622 hrs, Captain Laughton, who was just finishing his task in Sarajevo was contacted and briefed on the situation at S-1. He was told to position the TUA in such a manner as to block possible reinforcements coming up the main east -west road just south of S-1. He was also directed to be ready to fire at the tank anytime after targetting was confirmed.[37] Laughton acknowledged the task but indicated he had concerns about the minimum arming distance and the length of time he would be able to stay in a key location without attracting attention. He was told that once in location he was to act as if the vehicle had mechanical problems and indicate he would move out as soon as he could get the problem fixed. If he was unable to get the minimum arming distance he needed he was to pass the information over the company net as soon as possible.

As the conditions for success were being put into place, should a fight erupt at S-1, Captain Stutt was busy attempting to defuse the situation. Fortunately, he was able to convince the local military that both sides should lower their weapons to reduce tensions. Shortly after this the UN representative, Mike Challenger, arrived and after some additional discussions it was agreed that the UNHCR would be given the opportunity to produce the necessary papers.

In the meantime, the company reserve had arrived at the "S" bend and C/S 52, which had been told to turn around by the Serbs, were ordered by company headquarters to move back to the "S" bend to reinforce the reserve should the situation deteriorate further.[38]

At about 1650 hrs, C/S 55, the TUA, reached the area of S-1 and requested further direction. Captain Stutt indicated that although there was still some tension things were returning to a point where he was confident that he could handle the situation without resorting to force. So after a brief pause, C/S 55 was ordered to move through the checkpoint and go directly to the "S" bend to join the reserve. At 1800 hrs, the Serbs allowed C/S 51 to pass checkpoint S-1 and the reserve returned to camp.[39] Interestingly, as it was on its way back to camp, it passed the UN ready reserve consisting of only two Danish APCs.[40]

It was clear that once the TUA was in place, there was no question that had shooting started the company would have come out the winner. The main problem was that the tactical victory would have been the result of good luck rather then good planning. At the time of the incident, the UN was starting to force sensitive issues such as airspace control and the protection of safe areas like Srebrenica, and it was clear that the Serbs were tense. However, no special precautions were taken despite the change in the overall situation or the fact that this had translated to the local level with the presence of the T-54/55 at the checkpoint. The key lesson taken from this event was that even when conducting peacekeeping missions, military forces must always be ready for a fight.

To prevent a reoccurrence of this situation, convoys were reorganized to become more self-contained fighting units. When possible, TUAs and additional personnel were also allocated to the missions. More importantly, despite the pressure of taskings on the company, a reserve was always kept available.

Another important observation that came out of the incident at S-1 was the fact that Captain Stutt was put in a very difficult position and he performed extremely well. He was able to remain cool under volatile conditions and, despite the fact the Serbs appeared overwhelmed by events, he was able to control the circumstances and bring the situation back under control without resorting to the use of force. This event reinforces the fact that peacemaking operations are by nature very decentralized and this type of environment puts a huge burden on junior commanders. As a result, units need to put quality leaders up front. Equally important, those leaders need to know that the decisions they make will be fully supported by their chain of command.

The incident at S-1 brings out another point regarding support to humanitarian missions. While military forces supporting NGOs have substantial capabilities that can be converted to humanitarian purposes, it must be remembered that the military are not specialized in the delivery of relief services and have a number of limitations when dealing with the requirement for escalation of force. In these circumstances, military organizations are under constant pressure as they attempt to deal with competing demands. In this case, Captain Stutt had only two options available - to talk or fight his way out. Had he used lethal force, it is likely that the entire mission would have suffered and months of gains and good will would have been for naught. On the other hand, had he done nothing, he risked losing his credibility in the eyes of the local belligerent leader, his own troops and all the affected UN agencies and NGOs. Moreover, failure to act could have cost the entire mission its credibility as well. It is exactly this type of situation that has turned peacekeeping and peacemaking missions into the complex, volatile and ambiguous activities that they have become.

In summary, in any army, the purpose of "leadership" is to complete the mission. Unfortunately, today's military leaders are now being placed into the forefront of very complex peacekeeping and peacemaking operations in which their decisions could have national or international consequences.[41]   To be successful in the new environment, leaders must be able to adapt to new and multifaceted political, military and social realities and they must be able to put them into the context of their military actions.[42] The operational challenges faced by Kilo Company leaders and the solutions they were able to come up with during their 1992 deployment into Bosnia-Herzegovina bear witness to this fact.

The success of Kilo Company in overcoming some of the important issues of the new environment shows that it is possible for organizations to make the transition. However, to achieve success in this new environment, leadership styles must evolve to a more team-orientated participative approach where knowledge and experience are blended together to achieve common goals. During the initial deployment and subsequent operations in BH, the key to Kilo Company's success, when dealing with the constant change and ambiguity, was a direct result of the willingness of leaders to adapt to the requirements of the situation. This was accomplished because leaders were willing to fully exploit the physical and intellectual resources available within their command. More importantly, commanders on the ground were expected to use their initiative and make the decisions necessary to complete the mission. They did so knowing they had the full support of the chain of command.

ENDNOTES

1   Canada, *Officer Professional Development 2020* (Ottawa: Department of National Defence, 2000), 7-10.

2   Ibid.

3   Anthony Parsons, *From Cold War to Hot Peace/ UN Interventions 1947 – 1995* (London: Penguin Books, 1995), 222 – 223.

4   UNPROFOR was the primary UN peacekeeping force in both Croatia and Bosnia-Herzegovina between February 1992 and March 1995.

5   The original United Nations plan for Croatia was based on two requirements: The first was the withdrawal of the JNA from all of Croatia and the demilitarization of the UNPAs; and the second was focused on the continuing functioning of the existing local authorities and police, under United Nations supervision, pending the achievement of an

overall political solution to the crisis. BACKGROUND TO THE UNITED NATIONS PROTECTION FORCE in the Former Yugoslavia <http://www.un.org/Depts/dpko/dpko/co_mission/unprof_b.htm> (*Prepared by the Department of Public Information, United Nations - September 1996*) accessed 21 September 2005.

6   "Bosniaks (natively: Bo‰njaci) are South Slavs descended from those who converted to Islam during the Ottoman period (15th-19th century)." < http://en.wikipedia.org/wiki/Bosniaks.> Accessed 18 September 2005.

7   Parsons, 228-229.

8   UNITED NATIONS PROTECTION FORCE, Accessed 18 September 2005. The intent was to "create the conditions of peace and security required for the negotiation of an overall settlement of the Yugoslav crisis."

9   Ibid. "In June 1992, as the conflict intensified and extended to Bosnia and Herzegovina, UNPROFOR's mandate and strength were enlarged in order to ensure the security and functioning of the airport at Sarajevo, and the delivery of humanitarian assistance to that city and its environs. In September 1992, UNPROFOR's mandate was further enlarged to enable it to support efforts by the UNHCR to deliver humanitarian relief throughout Bosnia and Herzegovina, and to protect convoys of released civilian detainees if the International Committee of the Red Cross so requested. In addition, the Force monitored the "no-fly" zone, banning all military flights in Bosnia and Herzegovina, and the United Nations "safe areas" established by the Security Council around five Bosnian towns and the city of Sarajevo. UNPROFOR was authorized to use force in self-defence in reply to attacks against these areas, and to coordinate with the North Atlantic Treaty Organization (NATO) the use of air power in support of its activities. Similar arrangements were subsequently extended to the territory of Croatia. In December 1992, UNPROFOR was also deployed in the former Yugoslav Republic of Macedonia, to monitor and report any developments in its border areas which could undermine confidence and stability in that Republic and threaten its territory."

10   TQ 4 courses include such things a Driver Wheel, Driver Track, Reconnaissance Patrolman, Sniper, and Pioneer, etc.

11   Kilo Company was the BG's combat support company, which included mortar platoon, anti-armour platoon, pioneer platoon, reconnaissance platoon and a small headquarters element. The company's total strength was around 134 people. Although, pioneer and reconnaissance platoons were able to maintain their primary support functions to assist BG and UNPROFOR operations, mortar and anti-armour platoons were used for convoy escort, security and traffic control tasks.

12   For companies that set up independent camps it should be noted that normal camp administrative and security tasks required as significant amount (almost 30 percent) of the company's resources right from the start of the mission. Tasks will include everything from

kitchen and cleaning duties, construction of defensive fortifications, manning observation posts, controlling access at the main gate, maintenance and leave must also be factored into the resource requirements. There are no short cuts on this bill cutting support resources for operational tasks can be done for a few days; however, neglecting administrative needs will eventually bite a commander in the ass! The key to the company's ability to maintain effective operations while operationally stressed is to have solid administrative procedures set up within the camp from the day the company hits the ground. A good company second in command and support staff is critical if companies are expected to operate independently for extended periods.

13   During an interview Captain Stutt stated "This was new territory for us, we went in with nothing and in a very short time were able to establish procedures that for the most part worked." Interview with Captain Stutt, 8 November 2005.

14   UNITED NATIONS PROTECTION FORCE, "On 13 March 1993, three aircraft dropped bombs on two villages east of Srebrenica, before leaving in the direction of the Federal Republic of Yugoslavia (Serbia and Montenegro). UNPROFOR was not able to determine the identity of the aircraft and on 17 March, the Security Council strongly condemned all violations of its relevant resolutions underlining the fact that since early November 1992, the United Nations had reported 465 violations of the "no-fly zone". On 31 March, the Security Council adopted resolution 816 (1993), which extended the ban on military flights to cover flights by all fixed-wing and rotary-wing aircraft in the airspace of Bosnia and Herzegovina. Acting under Chapter VII of the Charter, the Council authorized Member States, to take, "all necessary measures" in the airspace of Bosnia and Herzegovina to ensure compliance with the ban on flights. On 9 April, the Secretary General of NATO informed the Security Council that the North Atlantic Council had adopted the "necessary arrangements" to ensure compliance with the ban on military flights and that it was prepared to begin the operations on 12 April 1993. As a result, operations authorized by resolution 816 (1993) started on 12 April at 12.00 GMT."

15   Parsons, 236.

16   UNITED NATIONS PROTECTION FORCE, "from the deployment of additional UNPROFOR battalions for this purpose in November 1992 until January 1993, a total of some 34,600 tons of relief supplies had been delivered to an estimated 800,000 beneficiaries in 110 locations throughout Bosnia and Herzegovina."

17   Toma provides a good account of the convoy organization the company used. "On the days that there were two convoys going into Sarajevo, Mortar Platoon had developed the following SOP for escorts. (I believe that this was put in place when Dennis Stutt was commanding the convoy duties, I took over when he went on leave) The escorts would depart in two packets, the first being of five APCs commanded by the Officer and the second packet of 3 APCs commanded by the Pl WO. Each escort packet would RV with their UNHCR truck convoys in Kiseljak and then head to Sarajevo. With five escorts, two APCs would lead, one APC would be in the middle of the convoy and two at the end. With

three APCs it was one, one and one. ***There were five regular UNHCR truck convoys that we escorted. Two British, one Danish and two made up of Bosnian drivers. UK1, UK2 and DK1 were modern 10 tonne trucks, 10 vehs to a convoy, that carried wheat flour for the bakery in Sarajevo. Most of the drivers were ex-military. Convoy Comd would ride in an armoured land rover. Bosnia 1 and Bosnia 2 were mixed trucks (8-10 vehs, don't remember for sure) that carried canned goods or other packaged food. If there were two convoys in a day, usually the first was of flour and the second a Bosnia one. However, that was not always the case and I do not know what the situation was on the day of the incident unless the logs mention the convoy name. The escorts would lead the convoy through a Croatian checkpoint (HV1?) and then through the first Serb checkpoint (Sierra 1), and then through Ilidza and the second Serb checkpoint (Sierra 3, an earlier checkpoint Sierra 2 was before Ilidza but was no longer manned) and then into the Sarajevo Airport. The convoy would circle the airport (in order to reposition by the entrance, ready to depart) and marry up with the UNHCR rep. Once we confirmed that the road into Sarajevo was open and everything was good to go (I think we did this two ways, the UNHCR rep checked on his net and we called UN Sarajevo HQ on our radios to confirm) then two APCs were despatched ahead to picquet areas of the road that had regular sniper activity. One position was facing a factory and the other a housing complex or something like that. Our picquets usually carried our own snipers with them as atts. At a set time after the first two APCs left (I remember it as 10 minutes) the escort commander led the convoy down to the PTT Bldg. The picquets fell in behind the convoy as it passed. At the PTT Bldg the trucks then separated from the convoy and moved to the bakery or warehouse on their own. The escort (all five APCs) circled the PTT Bldg and headed back to the airport. The escort always headed back to the airport to wait in case the road into Sarajevo got closed, the escort could still possibly leave for Kiseljak from the airport instead of being stuck at the PTT Bldg. At the airport, the two picquet APCs would marry up with the second convoy and they would repeat the procedure. Return trips would be done similarly. Five APCs would travel to the PTT Bldg to meet the convoy. (UNHCR rep at airport would inform us when the trucks were unloaded and ready to depart) After meeting up, the two picquet vehs would depart to their posns and then the convoy would follow. We did not put the picquets out on the way in to pick up the convoy in case there was a delay at the PTT Bldg and the picquets would be sitting in position for too long. Normally, the trucks would be waiting for us, three APCs would pull off and get in posn in the convoy and the picquet APCs would drive right by and head out to their posns. On the way back to the airport the picquets would fall in behind the convoy. At the airport, the convoy would circle around the terminal and the two picquets would detach to the second group of three APCs. Once confirmation is made that the road from the airport to Kiseljak was open then the first convoy would head out with three APCs as escort. The second escort - originally three APCs plus the two picquets - would then go pick up the second convoy when unloading was complete, go to the airport, circle the terminal, reorg and head out." Interview with Captain Mark Toma, 4 November 2005.

18   The PPT building was the old Sarajevo telephone exchange building being used by the UN as a Headquarters for Sector Sarajevo.

19   "K" Coy, communications log sheet entry, 0920 hrs, 25 March 1993, 2nd Battalion, The Royal Canadian Regiment, operations log book [henceforth "K" Coy Log], p. 2. serial 26.

20   K - Coy Log, 25 March 1993, p. 3. serial 48.

21   Captain Stutt stated that one of the SOPs [the platoon] put in place was unless [a soldier] had a reason to be outside his vehicle he stayed in it. And if he had to move from vehicle to vehicle he was to conduct his business in the vehicle he was visiting. He suggests "that this SOP more so than the rain contributed to the fact that there were no injuries." Interview with Captain Stutt, 8 November 2005.

22   K - Coy Log, 25 March 1993, p. 6. serial 67.

23   The Tarcin-Kresovo road was little more then a dirt track that had been carved out of the side of a hill. However, the road became critical to economic and military movement in the region when the Serb's cut the main east - west road from the coast into Sarajevo.

24   Todd Helmus, *Steeling the Mind Combat Stress Reactions and Their Implications for Urban Warfare.* (United States Army: contract No. DASW01-01-C-0003.), 128-129.

25   Ibid., 128-129. The report indicated that "while most soldiers with a prior episode of CSR do well once symptoms recede, others will go on to have a second reaction...It is consequently suggested that the U.S military adopt peer-mentoring programs that provide NCOs training in stress control as organic to maneuver units."

26   Parsons, 230-231. The military force that went into Srebrenica was Gulf Company Group from 2 RCR. Echo Company provided elements of AAP and Pioneers to support the mission but was not otherwise involved in the operations. It has been estimated that by March 1993, "in Srebrenica alone, thirty to forty civilians a day were dying of starvation, cold or lack of medical treatment."

27   On 09 April 1993, while on an IRM, Captain Laughton's vehicle received a total of 7 hits and he received a flesh wound. Fortunately, he was able to return to duty the following day.

28   Because of the heavy tasking load only five APCs could be sent to BH command. K - Coy Log, 24 April 1993. p. 8. serial 66.

29   TOW = Tube launched, Optically tracked, Wire guided – heavy anti-tank weapon system.

30   Laughton also indicated that although the TOW was the subject of some interest by Serb authorities no comments were made about the system.

31   K - Coy Log, 24 April 1993, p. 7. serial 55.

32   This was a regular occurrence. Any real or imagined violation or point of contention at one checkpoint involving any UN contingent would very quickly create problems for all UN traffic at any number of checkpoints.

33   According to the written After Action Report submitted by Captain Stutt "When C/S 51 arrived at S-1 the Dutch shuttle was still in place with a T-54/55 in location pointing both its main gun and its 14.5mm MG at the shuttle." "K" Coy, Convoy Report 056, 25 April 1993 paragraph 11.

34   K - Coy Log, 24 April 1993, p. 10. serial 74

35   K - Coy, Convoy Report 055, dated 25 April 1993, paragraph 11.

36   Ibid., 11.

37   Ibid, 11.

38   K - Coy Log, 24 April 1993, p. 11. serial 77.

39   K - Coy Log, 24 April 1993, p. 16. serial 109.

40   Captain Stutt believed he was successful at S1 only because of the quality of soldiers and NCOs he had with him. " There was a significant amount of initiative being displayed by the men under my command. Our training was validated, our debriefs and lessons learned were remembered as our internal SOPs kicked in, for example, if memory serves me correctly, even before we readied the weapons, my NCO knew what their assigned targets and arcs were. This included the MG, the main and x-ray houses. And although this was our first encounter with a tank at S1 if a shot were to be fired I knew where it would come from. In other words, as I was busy trying to diffuse the situation I was free to do so because the NCO were busy applying what they do so well, taking commander's intent and acting upon it. So as much as I could not predict what the Serbs would do, I was in control and, as you stated, confident that the situation could be resolved. For all their grandstanding the belligerent forces on the ground wanted a solution and I gave it to them. My offer to lower weapons was seen as genuine, especially in light of the fact that they knew I was also prepared to use force and my resolve on that day which was no different than any other day we went through that check point. ." Interview with Captain Stutt, 8 November 2005.

41   *Officer Professional Development 2020,* 7-10.

42   Bernard M. Bass, *Transformational Leadership.* (New Jersey: Lawrence Erlbaum Associates, Publishers, 1998), 3.

CHAPTER 4

LEADERSHIP ON OPERATIONS –
THE BASIC TRUTH ABOUT MAJORS

Colonel Jon Vance

Remarkably, little has been written on the subject of sub-unit command, a role which is largely held by majors in the Canadian Forces (CF). Sub-unit command is often seen as the main event in a major's career, and is therefore the focus of leadership and command training for those about to become, or who are already 'field officers' – the term the army uses to describe the level between junior and senior officers. What is perhaps even less discussed and indeed less celebrated is the general vice of the specific role that army majors play in a unit, particularly on operations. The aim of this chapter is to examine and elaborate on what it means to be a major in a unit deployed on operations. Keeping in mind that not all of them are unit are sub-unit commanders, I contend that there is a subtle but very important role that all the majors in a unit play regardless of their specific employment. In the end, I hope this chapter will be of use to those about to embark on operations as sub-unit commanders. In addition, it should serve to remind all that, regardless of employment, it is largely the cadre of majors in a unit that determines if a Commanding Officer's (CO) intent will be met, and therefore, they play a critical role in the level of success that the unit will achieve.

For the purposes of illustration, as well as the opportunity to slip in the occasional war story, the United Nations (UN) operational tour in Croatia conducted by the 1st Battalion, The Royal Canadian Regiment Battle Group (1 RCR BG) in 1994/95 will be used. Operation HARMONY, Rotation 5, CANBAT 1 – that's who we were, and I was the battalion operations officer (Ops O) and Officer Commanding (OC) Combat Support Company.

When asked to contribute to this work, I reviewed other treatises on leadership, many of which described the jobs and experiences of majors in a unit, most notably company command. They were, and will remain, a valuable contribution to leadership learning and will stand as essential pieces of history waiting to be used by future generations seeking to perfect their skills as officers and leaders.   This short chapter was developed as a result of my profound respect and admiration for those of my peers in the 1 RCR BG with whom I served in Croatia between October 1994 and April 1995.   In thinking back to that time, I realize that what I most want to convey in this chapter, and perhaps leave to history, is the overall effect on a unit and influence on its performance, well beyond the technical application of doctrinal skills and leadership, that a team of majors imparts.   In reality, I recognize that the influence of 'the majors,' was not all good. However, as the tour fades into memory, only the good parts remain vivid and those are the ones worth remembering.   As such, this is dedicated to my fellow majors on that tour; those fine officers from whom I learned so much.

Understanding that this volume will be read widely by all ranks of the CF, I owe a disclaimer right from the start. This work is not intended to glorify the rank, nor somehow make the cadre of majors appear more important than any other rank level in a battalion. We soldiers all know that it takes a team to make things work, and that the sergeants-major, the captains, the master-corporals and the privates all have vital parts to play. In the end, the battalion would cease to function if any one group performed poorly. Indeed, when it comes right down to it, the majors are perhaps the only group that could be plucked right out of the order of battle without too adversely affecting the unit's chance at success – such is the skill and training of our seconds-in-command. Taken a step further, it's probably true that the battalion could have performed just fine filled only with non-commissioned officers (NCOs) and private soldiers – so this is dedicated to them too, for they often made us majors look far better than we really were.

So what is this all about really?   I contend that the straightforward proximity that majors have, particularly in a unit on operations, with the commanding officer affords them the occasions to influence the CO, while at the same time they bear the responsibility to ensure the CO's influence is well projected throughout the unit. Put simply, they are the best placed to advise the CO (with the exception perhaps of the Regimental Sergeant-Major (RSM), but that appointment merits a book all of its own!). In addition, they are also best situated to fully understand, and therefore pass on, the CO's intent to their subordinates and sub-unit. Sounds simple, but the pressures of operations and the distraction of a million daily details can cloud these basic truths of the purpose of a major.

INFLUENCING THE CO

At this juncture it is worth qualifying the difference, and therefore the value of hoisting these basic truths aboard, between a unit on operations and one in garrison. On operations the stakes are higher, the details matter, and the consequences of failure to complete missions as outlined in orders are far greater. If a CO's intent is slightly misunderstood during garrison training, it results in a decent chance for a learning experience. Conversely, on operations, the same misunderstanding can result in catastrophe. The tempo of operations can also have the effect of numbing the senior leadership such that it succumbs to the 'tyranny of the present' and forgets it has a larger purpose beyond the myriad of daily details and tasks. If this longer-range (big picture) view and comprehension of the broader purpose or mission is not exercised, then the necessary relationship a CO has with his field officers is weakened and the unit suffers. If this happens in garrison it could go un-noticed, but on operations, with a unit living together 24/7, the effect can be profound.

The first of the three basic truths is that the majors are better placed to advise the CO than any other. While it is a privilege to do so, advising a CO while on operations bears with it tremendous responsibility. Advice can be offered in group settings, during a 'war cabinet' meeting for example, or individually. Either way, the CO relies upon his majors to help him think through challenges so they must remain sufficiently aware of the 'big picture' to be able to offer useful advice.

Major Kevin Robinson, Officer Commanding Charles Company ("C" Coy) was very good at this. His Area of Operations (AO) was particularly challenging in that the local (Krajina) Serb Commander was extremely difficult to deal with. Major Robinson's advice on how to deal with the situation was rendered privately, as well as during war cabinet meetings, and the overall effect was that the battalion was rarely caught off guard by belligerent action. In one instance, during a period when the belligerent forces thought they could restrict the movement of our forces, Major Robinson advised that we could retain freedom of movement by assertively exercising it at every opportunity. He was convinced that the local warlord and his forces would back down from confrontation. I found this advice particularly interesting for two reasons. First, it met the CO's intent of retaining freedom of movement while not recklessly endangering the safety of our troops. And second, it was the sort of advice that, had he been wrong, could have easily resulted in casualties. The CO, Lieutenant-Colonel Mark Skidmore, appeared to accept the advice, and issued the appropriate orders pertaining to how we were to deal with attempts at restricting our movement. As a result, our battalion enjoyed complete freedom of movement within our AO, and helped our flanking battalions regain some of theirs.

I offer this example to illustrate that, although the CO was fairly certain of the course of action he wanted pursued, it was the advice received in this instance that I believe satisfied him to the extent that he could issue orders with full confidence in the outcome. The thing about providing advice, again particularly on operations, is that it must be timely and it must be substantiated. This surely sounds like motherhood, but it is easy to forget. Operations are fast-paced, and the desire to make immediate decisions and issue orders is strong in our culture. One must be cautious about being too "off-the-cuff" about providing advice to a CO, even if it is solicited casually. At the same time, if an officer feels that he/she may have valuable advice to give, then it behooves him/her to either think and plan well ahead so that he/she is ready with advice when asked, or after being queried, seek sufficient time to think and render good advice. The absolute master of this was our Deputy Commanding Officer (DCO), Major Mike Jorgensen. Not one to be bullied, even by situations involving tremendous stress and pressure, his approach to providing advice was almost always to first figure out when the advice was really needed for decision-making. Once he determined the timelines, he then used the time available to best effect to research and prepare his advice.

I saw Major Jorgensen at his best following a brutal attack on two of our soldiers who were returning from an Observation Post (OP) on New Years Eve, 1994. The soldiers had been ambushed in their Iltis jeep by a group of Krajina Serb soldiers, and, as they were badly wounded, were being evacuated to Canada. The Sector Commander convened a meeting between Major Jorgensen, the Acting CO at the time, and the local commander responsible for the thugs who had ambushed our troops. Emotions were high, as one could imagine, and the Sector Commander was interested in determining what should be done. In the Sector Commander's office, just prior to meeting the Serb Commander, Jorgensen's advice was sought. He had clearly thought things through, and offered a thorough analysis and recommendations on how to proceed – including a strong effort to stiffen the Sector Commander's resolve in dealing forcefully with the Serbs. His efforts worked, and the situation was dealt with reasonably well – at least as well as one could expect in this sort of mission.

The value of this example, at least to me, was that in his capacity as Acting CO, Major Jorgensen represented the views and the approach one could imagine the CO himself taking. Moreover, by maintaining a consistent approach that the Sector Commander had become familiar with, because of his many dealings with his Canadian battle group, the Sector Commander was more inclined to accept Jorgensen's 'Acting' role with reasonable confidence.

To summarize here, Majors in a unit are often in the position of having to provide advice to the Commanding Officer, or even, as the example above showed, providing advice in his name. I contend that the most successful officers are ones that think through their advice thoroughly and understand the CO's overall intent, so their advice remains consistent and pertinent.

SPREADING THE CO'S INTENT

The second of the basic truths about majors is that they are generally best placed and sufficiently well informed, experienced and capable of ensuring the accurate passage of the CO's intent. In this instance I think it useful to distinguish between what we mean by CO's intent for a specific operation versus the CO's overall intent for the mission. I think we are all sufficiently well trained to capture and pass on a CO's intent for a specific tactical action – it is drilled into us from the beginning of our training. It has been my experience, however, that most COs will attempt, during the planning for an operational tour, to set the tone for the overall mission. This is a critical part of the CO's operational design for the duration of the tour.

It falls, therefore, to the CO's orders group (O Gp), particularly the majors, to maintain the tone throughout the mission, and to keep it in mind when issuing orders or indeed when providing advice. Although perhaps another blinding statement of the obvious, operational tours are long enough, and the tempo can be sufficiently demanding that the senior leaders can get distracted and lose the thread of the CO's overall intent.

A wise CO will use many opportunities to re-state his intent, and work to maintain the tone and climate he wants in the unit, but a good cadre of majors will make this easier and more personalized for subordinates. Another good example from Major Kevin Robinson illustrates this point. The CO had made it clear that his 'mission' intent included not allowing his forces to be bullied (such were the days of UN tours that this could be an issue), while avoiding escalation. On a fine spring day the local Krajina Brigade decided to deploy a sniper equipped with a Draganov rifle about 400 meters from Major Robinson's company compound. The sniper had clearly been deployed to harass and intimidate UN forces. Major Robinson's immediate reaction was to deploy a team of battalion snipers that were in location – very professional and intimidating in their own right. They made no show about it, but when they were set in their position on the roof of a building in the compound Major Robinson dispatched a small delegation to visit the offending sniper. With a translator, or perhaps just using the international signing for "if you shoot you'll die" the delegation pointed out the professionals on the roof. As I recall it took some time and a number of indications to even get the young man to see where his opposite numbers were. It became clear to him that he was in a losing situation, and he departed the location – leaving behind his rifle. All this was done without calls to the CO, and without any question of authority, Major Robinson had addressed the situation. Because he remained well within the CO's intent and all other constraints, he was successful and no further incidents of this nature materialized.

It is an art, I believe, to distill and be consistent with something as complex as a CO's intent or tone for an entire mission. It can change depending upon what happens during the mission, but the CO will expect all actions to adhere to it. It falls to the majors to put everything together so that it makes sense to their soldiers on a daily basis. This is not always easy, and I remember that we sometimes found ourselves in situations where it was difficult to explain our intended actions to our troops. But consistent and persistent efforts always paid off.

COHESIVENESS AND COOPERATION

The third and last basic truth about being a major is that one cannot perform one's job in the absence of teamwork, even when one is a field officer. Being a member of the senior leadership cadre in a unit on operations is demanding and places tremendous stress on individuals as well as on the leadership team. It is worth remembering that the field officers in a unit are usually 'large' personalities whose mood and working relationship with the other senior leaders is watched closely by their subordinates and by key staff in unit headquarters. Poor cohesiveness and cooperation between the senior leaders can lead to distrust within the unit and potentially a lack of confidence in those demonstrating less than cooperative characteristics.

Depending on the type of mission and the deployment footprint of the unit, sub-unit commanders can find themselves physically isolated from each other and from unit headquarters. Physical isolation can lead to emotional and psychological isolation if the senior leaders have not developed good working relationships amongst each other – worse yet, in instances where psychological isolation occurs, a 'we-they' attitude can develop that affects the whole sub-unit. It is important, therefore, that the leadership team develops mutual respect and a desire to work together to solve problems rather than allow themselves and their sub-units to adopt a siege mentality fostered by feelings of isolation.

Finally, although it is an issue that is rarely addressed, while the peer group for senior leaders in a unit may be small, it is vitally important to help deal with stress and to foster confidence in each other. 'Lonely at the top' is an expression one comes to accept with each step up in the hierarchy of a unit, yet the stress of commanding, supporting or planning operations – the usual roles of unit field officers – requires the development of a certain reliance on peers in order to better endure the high tempo of operations. It is critical, therefore, to become familiar with being a member of a leadership team where cohesiveness and cooperation are critical. The earlier in your career that you realize this and practice it, the better you will be served as you advance in rank.

CHAPTER 5

KEEPING PEACE AND FREEDOM IN BOSNIA: DRVAR 1998[1]

Lieutenant-Colonel Howard Coombs

I don't know who was looking over us that day. We were waiting for the moment when this thing would turn into a bloodbath.[2]

Howard G. Coombs

On 4 August 1995, Operation Storm was initiated by Croatia to regain control of the Krajina region, occupied by secessionist Serbians since 1991. In the face of an organized and intense military onslaught as many as 200,000 Croatian Serbs left this area. It was later opined by the President of Croatia, Francis Tudjman, that these rebel Serbs had "disappeared ignominiously, as if they had never populated this land. We urged them to stay but they did not listen to us. Well then, bon voyage."[3] As if in fulfilment of these words the depopulated Serbian villages and farms were soon occupied by new Croatian inhabitants. The town of Drvar was in a region of Bosnia affected by Croatia's military efforts and was similarly affected.

Prior to this offensive, Drvar had a population of over 17,000 persons of Bosnian Serbian ancestry. However, Operation Storm prompted those Serbs to abandon Drvar, with little notice, leaving much of its infrastructure intact. These buildings were soon taken over by about 7,000 displaced Bosnian Croatians.[4] Although the General Framework Agreement for Peace in Bosnia and Herzegovina, colloquially known as the Dayton Accords was signed within months of Operation Storm and guaranteed the right of Serbs to come back to this area few returns occurred. It was not until the NATO Stabilization Forces (SFOR) mission in 1997, that any significant pressure commenced to relocate dispossessed former Serbian residents of Drvar back to their homes.[5] However, this right of return proved difficult to exercise.[6] Croatians who had left their own homes elsewhere, moved to Drvar and had now re-established themselves and improved their new residences were not going to permit the former Serbian owners to regain and reoccupy those properties. They would do everything in their power to resist any attempt at reoccupation.

Exacerbating these challenges was the number of local forces supporting disintegrating activities. Garrisoning the town was the 1ˢᵗ (*Ante Bruno Busic*) Brigade *Hrvatsko Vijece Odbrane* (Bosnian Croatian Army – HVO) accompanied by their families.[7] This undersized formation was at most several thousand soldiers equipped with small arms and capable of rudimentary low-level infantry tactics. Despite being designated an armour brigade, it had little in the way of mechanized vehicles or trained crews and, while ostensibly compliant, they were believed to be involved with disobedient local elements and working closely with the *Hrvatska Demokratska Zyednica* (Croatian Democratic Party - HDZ). The local HDZ, with its strong ties to Croatia, agitated openly to further the goal of a greater Croatia. This party controlled local politics and was linked to a Croatian wood processing firm, the Finvest Corporation.[8] Finvest was the only large scale company in the region, offering employment to Bosnian Croats willing to move to Drvar. During our tenure in the area they did not hire Serbian returnees.

Local politics added further tension to the area because while the municipal office holders were for the most part Croatian, the Mayor, Mile Marcetta, and a proportion of the council, were Bosnian Serbian. This situation was created as a result of the elections of September 1997 that permitted not only the current Croatian inhabitants of the town to exercise their franchise but also the displaced Serbian inhabitants. The result was in all respects a truly Balkan outcome, with the Mayor and his Serbian council members sporadically visiting the town only by means of International Community (IC) and SFOR assistance and security.[9] The resultant friction between the two ethnic groups was enormous. For example, the Deputy Mayor was not only Croatian but also the local head of the HDZ. He occupied the Mayor's office and disregarded any initiatives by Serbian municipal officials to participate in local governance unless the IC exerted pressure to comply. Despite these challenges, Marcetta assisted the United Nations High Commission on Refugees (UNHCR) by encouraging Serbian Displaced Persons, Refugees and Evacuees (DPREs) to move back to the district.

It was into this complex environment that the men and women of the 1ˢᵗ Battalion, The Royal Canadian Regiment Battle Group (1 RCR BG) commenced their deployment in Bosnia-Herzegovina (BH) as part of Canada's Operation Palladium commitment. The mission was "to provide a secure environment necessary for continued peace."[10] The SFOR camp at Drvar was somewhat isolated; over two hours by road from the Headquarters at Coralici and about the same distance from the other elements of the BG at Zgon. Drvar was garrisoned by the Charles Company Group, a robust infantry-based organisation that was normally about 200 strong. Within those numbers there was a 119 person infantry company and representatives of all elements and trades that would allow the Company and the Camp to function efficiently. It should be noted that once the leave plan commenced during the mission these numbers could, at times, dwindle to half of this.[11] Additionally, there were a number of BG detachments, like anti-armour, that were more or less permanently stationed in Drvar, as well as, an American-led NATO Civil Military Cooperation (CIMIC) team and a small group from the United States Army who managed the SFOR radio station, *Radio Mir*.[12] This station broadcast music and news with an orientation that supported the overall SFOR mission.

With increasing pressure from the Office of the High Representative (OHR) and others to cooperate with resettlement, accept Marcetta and his council, as well as integrate Bosnian Serbians into the local police force, the Bosnian Croatian community made little public show of resistance.[13] However, they manifested their resistance in other ways. Normally, an escalating scale of violence commenced with threats and intimidation, arson, violence, and to the most extreme case, murder.[14] The Charles Company Group, after a superb transition with the Reconnaissance Squadron of Lord Strathcona's Horse (Royal Canadians) commenced operations with aggressive mechanized and dismounted patrolling.[15]

We were for the most part well-prepared for this mission. Our earlier pre-deployment training had been conducted over a six-month period and stressed types of military operations that we could potentially be involved in, from humanitarian to combat operations. On the other hand, it soon became clear that we lacked counter insurgency training, particular techniques for information gathering and analysis within an environment that had an indiscernible threat entity. The BG attempted to remedy this deficiency by providing a British sergeant who had served multiple tours in Northern Ireland to brief us on potential techniques. Lamentably, he destroyed his credibility amongst the Non-Commissioned Officers (NCO) and soldiers, by being apprehended, obviously quite drunk, within the camp area soon after he arrived. The idea that a senior NCO, regardless of nationality, would violate regulations concerning consumption of alcohol was unacceptable to the Canadian NCOs. As a result, any later attempts for him to educate the company fell on deaf ears and we learned through trial and error.

As incidents of local resistance began to swell in January and February the actions of the 1 RCR BG became the centre of attention for the international community, NATO and SFOR Headquarters. Efforts to become networked into the Croatian community, and effect change from within, met with little success. This, coupled with mounting pressure from outside actors to produce results must have produced incredible pressure at the BG Headquarters, but none was transmitted to the Company Group. Sadly, after each incident, once the situation had stabilized and security levels were reduced incidents of violence against Serbs would resume.

A number of local, BG and Divisional operations were conducted in an attempt to discourage violence against Serbian returnees.[16] Operation Nero, in early February, was an example of one such effort and encompassed an enormous amount of resources, outside support and numerous visits. It was later described tongue in cheek by the Company Administrative Officer, Captain Scott McCorquodale:

The unseasonably warm weather during this time of the year resulted in an increase in displaced persons and refugees returning to the homes they occupied before the war…There were more house fires than the Los Angeles riots. We responded with everything we had and the population of the camp grew by over 30%. OP[ERATION] NERO involved increased patrolling and difficult hours for the platoons. The operation was particularly memorable for two reasons. Once the Div[ision] Comd [Commander] decided that the operation was going to be the main effort, assets started to come out of the woodwork. Among the items devoted to our cause were several helicopters, one equipped with a "Night Sun" [an extremely powerful searchlight] and a P3 Spy plane monitoring the town of Drvar constantly. The second reason this operation was so memorable was the unprecedented number of high-ranking visitors who adopted an intense interest in the area. Among such notable guests were the Supreme Allied Commander Europe. If we enjoyed anything about his visits it was watching his security flop around trying to look cool in front of the soldiers.[17]

It was during this period of increased Serbian returns that Charles Company was visited by the Sector Head for the UNHCR, who advised me that returnees would soon be introduced into the centre of town.

However, because many displaced Serbians were afraid of possible reactions by the Croatian majority this would only constitute a small fraction of the overall returns. Previously, the UNHCR had encouraged returnees to re-settle homes surrounding or on the fringes of Drvar and avoided potential conflict that could result in mixing Serbians into the Croatian population. The Sector Head believed that violence could be prevented if he had his fieldworkers live with these encircled returnees to ensure their protection.[18] However, the Sector Head also candidly admitted that by doing this he intended to provoke conflict and, consequently, a resolution. By putting these fieldworkers in harm's way he was also making SFOR take an aggressive stance against the resistant Croatians.[19]

I immediately informed him that levels of violence tended to escalate too quickly for SFOR to be contacted and respond before an aggressive act had occurred. He dismissed these comments, as well as those suggesting he was creating a situation that might result in the serious injury or death of one of his people. The next day I visited the local fieldworkers, provided them a realistic appraisal of the SFOR response capabilities in Drvar and recommended they consider carefully any UNHCR direction to place themselves in such a risky situation. They concurred and refused such direction when it did arrive. Unhappily, it did not make the SFOR contingent at Drvar a favourite of the Sector Head, who would later attribute difficulties with Serbian returns to a lack of local SFOR support.

Soon after this, it was announced that 1 Guards Brigade would be removed from their barracks in the middle of town, which had been Serbian apartments prior to the Croatian offensive. It was planned to reintroduce a large number of returnees to that area. While the HVO moved from that vicinity, into other locales around town, tension began to build. Fortunately, 1 Guards Brigade displaced themselves without incident.

Nonetheless, displays of SFOR determination continued. Operation Nero was followed in early April by Exercise Dynamic Response that deployed NATO's strategic reserve to the Drvar area of operations. About 200 American Marines and a platoon of Polish Airborne soldiers were sent to the area in a demonstration of NATO resolve and deployment capabilities. They stayed from 1 to 3 April, established patrol bases and assisted in patrolling the town before returning to their parent units.[20]

Immediately after this exercise about 180 Serbian returnees were placed in the now empty apartment building complex, which included several small warehouse type buildings, one of which had been a school. One structure became a storehouse for UN relief supplies and the school acted as the barracks for what evolved into a permanent SFOR security presence. Operation Hamlyn saw most of the 1 RCR BG operating in the area. Nonetheless, hostility was palpable from the Drvar Croatians.

Regrettably, efforts to reduce the intimidation, harassment and arson were not successful. During the Easter weekend, on 9 April, the OHR conducted a ceremony marking the occasion of the Serbian returns and had a large press conference. This acted to goad the local Bosnian Croatians and immediately afterwards there was a noticeable rise in the number of confrontations between local Croatians and SFOR troops. These ranged from simple taunting to speeding cars deliberately making close passes at foot patrols, all attempting to provoke a disproportionate response.

Finally, on 16 April two elderly Serbs were murdered about 500 metres from the front gates of the Company Group Camp and their home set alight. This Serbian couple had moved nearby about the beginning of April and, while not part of the main UNHCR movement into Drvar they had taken advantage of what they perceived from afar to be commencement of a the overall return of the Serbian population. They were quickly disabused of that notion when they returned to their own home and the Croatian occupant offered bodily harm if they pressed their claim against him. Instead they occupied a nearby vacant house, which had apparently belonged to their son. The local UNHCR representative requested that SFOR put a permanent guard on these returnees to ensure their safety. Given the security situation and the consideration that an enduring presence would engage about a third of my active patrolling effort I declined, but directed these returnees be incorporated into local patrol plans and checked regularly. Sadly, that was not enough and a double shooting and arson ensued:[21]

Around 160100Apr98 31B [Patrol Radio Callsign], commanded by MCpl Turcotte, and 31W commanded by Sgt Paris noticed a house fire during [the] course of a patrol. From previous patrols in the area they suspected that particular house to be occupied by an elderly Bosnian-Serb couple. As the two Patrol Commanders, accompanied by Pte Stymiest approached the house they noticed that someone had attempted to set the house ablaze at the front entrance. They immediately entered the ground floor and began searching for occupants. They soon found the body of the elderly gentleman, and shortly thereafter found the body of his wife. They continued to search the house for survivors. Locked doors impeded their search and eventually they retreated to the exterior of the building. Upon reaching the exterior MCpl Turcotte ordered his soldiers to fight the fire. At this point Ptes Stymiest and Kelson scaled an external staircase armed with an axe and a vehicle fire extinguisher. They attempted to extinguish the blaze, which was started on the second floor, for about 5 minutes. When it became evident that the fire was out of control, MCpl Turcotte ordered the extraction of the bodies from inside the house. At this point MCpl Turcotte, Ptes Kelson, Weiss and Stymiest re-entered the burning house and saved the bodies from being burnt by bringing them outside. Then this same group searched the rooms in the house that were previously left unchecked, by circling the exterior and looking through the windows. Only when they were certain that no further victims were left in the house did they discontinue their search. Throughout the entire ordeal Sgt Paris sent thorough and concise SITREPS [Situation Reports] to c/s 3 [company headquarters].[22]

The Duty Officer, Captain McCorquodale, consolidated the various reports and woke me to brief the distressing event. We continued with our normal operations, ensured all patrols understood what had transpired and exercised increased vigilance. Once I had confirmed that no other incidents had transpired I informed the Acting Commanding Officer (A/CO), Major Greg MacCallum, of the situation and this process continued until SFOR Headquarters in Sarajevo received notification.[23] Reaction by both military and non-military agencies was swift. Many elements of the BG returned to the area and the Special Representative of the UN Secretary General in Bosnia, Jacques Kline, flew to Drvar that day. He immediately escalated the tension in the area by firing some of the key Croatian officials in the town, including the Deputy Mayor. This was done in a very melodramatic fashion at the site of the murder, during an overcast and wet spring day, while standing over the corpses.

It was at this time that Kline, demanded the Company provide a military vehicle and crew to take the bodies to Sarajevo. I was extremely reluctant to do this as without clearances the movement of a military vehicle across so many boundaries would be extremely difficult. Additionally, from a practical point of view, I could spare neither the vehicles nor crews, as it would take at least two vehicles and four people for such a movement. Concurrently Kline telephoned numerous personages to arrange for a CNN team, preferably a prominent newscaster, Christianne Amanpour, to come to the location. Moreover, he telephoned the Supreme Allied Commander Europe (SACEUR), General Wesley Clark, to brief him and gain support for the movement of the bodies. Kline then handed the telephone to me with the words, "SACEUR wants to speak with you." My conversation with General Clark was brief and to the point. We had met recently during his visit to Drvar and he remembered that meeting. General Clark voiced his confidence in the BG to deal with anything that occurred and told me that he would not provide me any orders, as it was not his position to do so. I thanked him for that and we ended the call cordially.

Later that afternoon, when we received word that CNN would be unable to travel to town, I convinced Kline to co-opt a Croatian ambulance to drive the bodies to Sarajevo. He accepted the argument that the steel bed of an army truck would not be a fitting manner to convey the victims of this heinous crime. After obtaining a couple of body bags from the Acting Company Quartermaster Sergeant, Master-Corporal Jim Blackmore, two American Special Forces soldiers, who were Joint Commission Observers (JCOs), and I managed, with some difficulty, to fit the stiffened bodies into these surrogate caskets.[24] Later that evening Kline and his personal staff departed unmindful of the further escalation that he had precipitated.

I then contacted the A/CO, who had remained in Corilici, and briefed him on the events of the day. Soon a large portion of the BG was sent to Drvar to provide increased security. After a week the BG reduced its presence with the last elements departing early on 24 April. The BG Mortar Platoon remained, co-located with the greatest concentration of the Serbian returnees in the apartment complex at the centre of town. This location had the designation W/H/153.[25]

That day, without warning hundreds of the Croatian residents of Drvar rioted. They attacked the Serbian Mayor, Marcetta, and destroyed the offices and vehicles of many International Organizations (IO), Private Volunteer Organizations (PVO) and Non-Governmental Organizations

(NGO). The mob attempted to attack the Serbian returnees in the centre of town but was prevented from doing so by Canadian troops. Gradually, over the next 24 hours, the violence subsided and SFOR regained control. Serbian returnees who wished to leave were given the option to do so. Many chose this option and were escorted from the area in the following days.

I was initially informed of a disturbance in Drvar near midday 24 April, as the command group, Company Sergeant Major (CSM) Derek Ingersoll and myself, with our interpreter, Irena Drilo, and driver, Corporal Glen Patay, were returning in an armour vehicle from a liaison meeting with an adjoining British unit. As the reports were passed over the company radio net of a small disturbance at the city offices and nearby UN offices, I dispatched a patrol to observe and report. This small element, in an armoured vehicle, commanded by Sergeant D.E. Fischer moved to a nearby location where they could comply with my instructions. Also, of some concern was the fact that the Bosnian Serbian Mayor was in town that day with an IC escort to meet with the Croatian members of the municipal council.

From their reports I soon realized that this was no longer a minor protest but a large and destructive riot with IC buildings and vehicles on fire. I passed orders to the company headquarters to inform all international personnel to move to the Canadian camp.[26] A well-understood Multinational Division (Southwest) (MND (SW)) contingency plan, entitled Op Medusa, existed. This plan provided for a planned evacuation of all IC representatives to local camps and facilities if there was significant threat. While knowing that the authority to invoke Medusa lay with the Divisional headquarters I ordered local commencement of the operation, because it was grasped to a greater or lesser extent by all involved and would promote clarity of thought in the midst of confusion.[27] At this time I directed Sergeant Fisher and the Quick Reaction Force (QRF) section, which had joined him in another armoured vehicle, to assist with the evacuation of any international personnel in that area.[28]

With great courage and efficiency they moved their vehicles through the crowd and collected any IC workers in the buildings and removed them from the scene. Luckily, the CIMIC team was also manning their office in that location and used their armoured High-Mobility, Multipurpose Wheeled Vehicle (HUMVEE) to evacuate any people not taken by the

Charles Company vehicles. I was later surprised at the amount of damage this armoured HUMVEE sustained during this evacuation.[29]

We continued to edge our vehicle closer to a point where the violence could be observed. Flames climbed at least a hundred metres in the air from the small international complex across from the Town Hall. A large crowd of men and boys were moving back and forth, some drinking, many carrying sticks and throwing rocks. At this time 10 to 20 rioters attacked a fire truck manned by Serbian returnees that had arrived.[30] They smashed the window of the vehicle and attempted to strike the occupants with sticks, rocks and bottles. "You better be loading that machine gun," I urged CSM Ingersoll and instructed him to point it towards the attackers. But, even today I suspect he was already ahead of me and did not require encouragement.

The leader of the rioters noticed the CSM's actions and warned the others who moved away from the cab of the vehicle, which allowed the fire truck to make a hasty retreat from the area. The Serbian driver and fire fighting crew had sustained a number of non life-threatening injuries, but were able to return to the protection of the enclave at W/H/153.

At this point in time I believed all internationals had been evacuated and there was nothing to gain by remaining at this location. My immediate thought was to move the rest of the Mortar Platoon elements from W/H/153 to the Camp and then I suddenly remembered the 180 or so Serbians, who I had forgotten in the heat of the moment, were in the same area. I immediately realized that their protection would be of the utmost importance this day and attempted to obtain a coherent picture of what was occurring with the Serbians in and outside the town. It seemed as if mortar platoon had acted with decisiveness and evacuated all Serbians to the school location in the centre of W/H/153, but a crowd of hundreds were gathering and starting to burn apartment buildings and destroy vehicles. I suddenly received a report of an impacting mortar round at that location, which increased the urgency to reinforce this small group. Later, I realized that this message had been prompted by an exploding vehicle gas tank, heard by the radio operator secluded within the command post. Simultaneously patrols outside the town reported no disturbances. It was at this time I decided to move back to the Camp, muster my forces and issue orders.

While driving through the crowd towards the camp, members of the riot attempted to climb on our vehicle but were unable to seize a handhold due to its movement. As we were about to break free of the mob a Croatian policeman shouted something to my interpreter. Irena told me that the Serbian Mayor had been attacked and was thought to be dead. Then she indicated a location on the fringe of the riot where the body was supposed to be lying. I looked in that direction and saw at about 75 metres what could have been a pile of rags that were vaguely human in appearance. Unwilling to believe the Croatian policeman, Irena finally convinced me. I was very reluctant to risk the vehicle and its crew to make an attempt to pick up what was probably a corpse, however, we did so. In my mind it was a moral obligation and our duty to ensure that we made all efforts to recover him.[31] With little room to spare, our vehicle, pursued by the mob, speedily covered the distance to the body. We dropped our rear ramp and picked up what appeared to be the extremely bloody corpse of the Mayor, who had been severely beaten about the head. On the way to the Camp Irena realized Marcetta was tenaciously clinging to life. She began to yell that he was alive! I sent a radio message to my Command Post at the Camp to have the Medical Station prepared to assist the Mayor. I also ordered that the leadership components of all elements, including visiting or transiting groups, be in the conference room waiting for my orders.[32]

In the few minutes before I arrived at my headquarters and issued orders there were a number of significant considerations. Now realizing the scale of the violence, I was troubled for the two hundred or so Serbian returnees in the town, now guarded by an under strength Mortar Platoon. I believed they were at the greatest risk. Thus, the majority of the available combat soldiers would have to be committed to reinforce that platoon. I would need to evacuate to the Camp all international workers in the area, as well as provide for Camp defence. It was also necessary to provide some degree of protection to the returnees elsewhere in and around the town and there was neither a great deal of time, nor a large number of people to accomplish this.

The greatest dilemma posed during the initial stages of this incident was the order of protection. The prioritization was based on my understanding of the situation and interpretation of the rules of engagement (ROE) in effect at that time. Under those ROE, deadly force could be utilized because these ongoing events met the criteria for the use of force up to and including deadly force for each of the four separate situations listed in the

ROE. These were: to defend persons; protect mission essential property, such as the vehicles, weapons and communications equipment; to prevent serious crimes against others, in situations such as, against hostile forces attempting to prevent SFOR from discharging its duties; and in self-defence. The challenge for Canadians was that we neither possessed non-lethal systems, nor had national authorization to use them if they were given to us. Thus, for us, the intervening distance between non-lethal and lethal force was short.

Keeping this in mind I believed that those at most danger were the Serbian returnees in the centre of Drvar, followed by returnees on the exterior of town, and members of IOs, NGOs, and PVOs. All personnel and resources available would be necessary to meet those demands in that precedence and at the time I realized that this ordering was a calculated risk to save lives. Regrettably, this later had unintended consequences because agencies that had been working in Drvar abandoned their efforts due to their perception of it as a non-secure environment. I now believe that specific communications with these agencies regarding ROE and security issues, prior to the violence may have mitigated some of the effects of my decisions.

As we drove towards the Camp I could see large numbers of international aid workers moving on foot towards the front gates carrying various oddments of personal belongings. The analogy that immediately sprang to mind was sepia sketches I had reviewed depicting Napoleon's retreat from Moscow. Entering the main gate I perceived that the Camp had been galvanized into action, with personnel and vehicles prepared or being prepared for movement. We drove to the Medical Station, which was next to the Command Post, and quickly offloaded Marcetta. I told the CSM we needed a radio operator and that we would be departing the Camp as soon as I could pass coherent direction to the Company.

Ironically, as we handed the Mayor over to the medics we were being watched by a visiting group of Mayor and Reeves from the Ottawa valley. This group was touring the Canadian mission in Bosnia-Herzegovina to obtain a sense of what Canadian troops were doing in the region. From their wide-eyed stares at Marcetta's immobile form one could ascertain that they certainly were getting much more than they had anticipated.

I rushed upstairs to the Command Post, which consisted of a couple of rooms and included a communications suite of radio, Motorola and telephone. Most of the available leadership was there and direction was quickly passed. I would depart with the greatest portion of personnel, to reinforce the platoon at W/H/153, securing the Serbian area inside Drvar. Some troops, under command of Warrant Officer (WO) Mike Graham, our Transport NCO, were sent to warn and assist the members of different organisations to move to the Canadian Base Camp. Lieutenant Rob McBride, with the remainder of his platoon, was sent to patrol the exterior of Drvar and warn the Serbian returnees of the events occurring in the town.[33] By drafting all available NATO personnel in the vicinity to assist with these missions and the security of the camp perimeter all tasks were completed. I told my Acting Company Second-in-Command, Captain McCorquodale, to account for all members of the IC in the area and make provision for their stay with us.[34]

After quickly taking questions and affirming my confidence in all we departed within moments of finishing my very concise direction. As my vehicle left the Camp I was unsure of how many troops that I actually had with me. Our crew had increased by one, as CSM Ingersoll had dragooned Corporal Shawn Nobles, from our Company Command Post, to act as my radioman. What's more, I later found out that the bus bringing back a number of our personnel from leave had just arrived and these soldiers had got off the leave bus and into the backs of armour vehicles to follow me to W/H/153. It is a testament to them and the leadership of the company that this was done without any difficulty and little confusion.

Upon our arrival at the site we could see a crowd of hundreds of frenzied Croatians attempting to penetrate the slim perimeter the mortar platoon had established around the school in which the Serbian returnees were secured. Our small column of vehicles sped towards the building and a number of people moved to physically block us from attaining that goal. Corporal Patay, continued to drive but asked me what we wanted to do, I ordered him to increase speed and run them over if they got in our way. I knew if we stopped our undersized group of vehicles would be swarmed very quickly unless we used our weapons, something I wished to avoid. Much to his credit Patay just nodded, "put the pedal to the metal" and people flew away from the front of our speeding vehicle. It takes a great deal of courage to stay in front of tons of speeding metal and luckily none of the rioters took up the challenge.

We pulled in next to the school and assumed on-site command from the Mortar Platoon Commander, Captain Brian Bedard, who provided me with a brief synopsis of events. I am still amazed at what they had accomplished in a short period. The few Canadian troops in that location had been able warn and move almost two hundred Serbians into the school. Importantly they were able to do this and provide protection, while greatly outnumbered and without shooting anyone. Bedard advised me that a number of warning shots had been fired and quickly explained their circumstances. These were the first but certainly not the last shots to be fired that day.[35]

I also took stock of the numbers of personnel we had available. There was a total of about fifty, including the Mortar Platoon, those Charles Company soldiers who had accompanied me on my dash from the Camp, the Delta Company Quartermaster Sergeant, WO George Laidlaw, and his staff, as well as two British dog handlers and their dogs, although only one dog team was functioning.[36] At that point I had CSM Ingersoll ensure the perimeter was reinforced and moved further out from the school. This perimeter consisted of armed soldiers standing at 5 metre intervals in a semicircle around the back of school while the remainder of the soldiers occupied the front of the school blocking the mob that was trying to enter through windows and doors.[37]

Bedard took me for a tour of the school and I saw that a number of attempts to set fire to it using diesel fuel had occurred, and there were ongoing attempts to enter through windows and doors. I positioned the remaining dog team inside with instructions to use the dog to attack anyone that entered the building. I also ordered Bedard to explain to his soldiers they were to shoot anyone that attempted to set fire to the building and anyone that succeeding in getting by the dog.[38] It was at this time I noticed that despite the rapidity with which events were taking place time seemed to slow down, as did all the activities that were occurring. It was a surreal sensation but worked to my advantage.

Once I exited the building I sent a quick report to McCorquodale and thought of the immediate challenges. I knew that given the level of violence it was probable that incidents of lethal force would occur. Though the pre-deployment training package had stressed application of the ROE and provided many practical individual and collective scenarios including a riot, I felt that it was necessary to reaffirm to the dispersed elements of the Company Group the need for proportionality, restraint and the inherent right of self-defence. Firstly, in order to communicate this intent to everyone, I sent a radio transmission on the company net to all stations and subordinate commanders were told to pass my words to their soldiers. Secondly, I inspected the entire perimeter and spoke to every soldier in the immediate vicinity to reiterate this intent. The violence seesawed back and forth for some time but the constant re-affirmation of intent and a challenging ROE pre-deployment package assisted in avoiding an application of lethal force. Given the historical tradition of resistance to armed authorities, killing a civilian would have violently turned the Croatian ethnic communities throughout the region against SFOR and created an insurgency in the Drvar area. This would have been an unsolvable dilemma for SFOR.

After my tour of the hastily improvised defences I received notification from McCorquodale that almost all members of the IC had been accounted for and the CIMIC team and others were assisting in tallying all Serbians throughout the area. Bedard believed we had evacuated all the returnees from the surrounding and now burning apartment buildings, but was not sure. We had suffered no serious injuries or deaths.

Suddenly, a message arrived from McCorquodale saying there were five members of ITI – Impact Teams International – trapped in one of the burning apartment buildings by the mob. They were communicating by cellular telephone with one of their colleagues in the Camp, who was in turn speaking with McCorquodale, and so, in a convoluted manner, we managed to pinpoint their location. I sent WO Laidlaw and a section commanded by Master-Corporal D.L. Byard to rescue them. I must admit I experienced a degree of nausea as I watched the vehicle, with closed hatches, slowly move through the crowd toward the smouldering buildings. So much could go wrong. They were followed by a sizable group pelting their vehicle with rocks and bottles. As the armoured vehicle neared the main doors of the correct structure it turned and backed into the entrance, blocking that entry from the mob and allowing the soldiers to use the combat doors in the back of vehicle to enter the building, where they found the five ITI workers. They made a return trip to our location under the same hostile conditions as the original crossing. Re-entering our perimeter through a laneway between the school and the small warehouse they were followed by the rioters. Quickly unloading the shocked aid workers Ingersoll moved them into the school with the returnees.

I remained outside overseeing the deployment of Byard's section to close off the laneway and eliminate the opening in our perimeter.

The rioters remained at the other end of the laneway throwing projectiles of various types. I moved into the open and hunched my helmet into the neckpiece of my Kevlar vest to keep an eye on the proceedings. One youngish man was obviously agitating the group to hurry up the alleyway and enter our perimeter. As he started to run towards me I drew my pistol and made a show of chambering a round, I then raised my hand to indicate "STOP!" but with little effect. Aiming at his onrushing form, emotionlessly and without hesitation, I started to squeeze the trigger, but quickly realized I had not fired a warning shot. With fractions of a second to spare I dropped my arm, fired a round into a strip of dirt about a metre from him, then returned my pistol to its original position and awaited his reaction. The man stopped and backed off, as did the following crowd. Bizarrely enough they started to applaud, recommenced throwing projectiles, then promptly looted and set fire to the small neighbouring building being used as a UN storage facility for aid supplies. Another effort was later made to breach the perimeter in this area but Ingersoll, in a similar manner, fired his pistol and arrested the attempt.

While the crowd was occupied with the warehouse I readjusted the perimeter and sent Laidlaw, with Byard's section to check all the now smoking buildings for any returnees we may have missed. In most cases the top floors had suffered significant damage but the bottom parts seemed mostly intact. Laidlaw, Byard and the section spent the next hour or two avoiding the mob and conducting this risky building to building search. They found no other returnees. I found it hard to believe only about two hours had passed since the initial report of a disturbance.

Soon after, two American JCOs, who had forced their civilian vehicle through the crowd, joined our small group. Almost simultaneously with their arrival a British light observation helicopter that had been observing and reporting the riot, told me over the radio they had spotted an individual with a long barrelled weapon, which they thought was an automatic rifle.[39] The JCOs, overhearing the radio transmission, immediately informed me they were a qualified sniper team; their rifle was in the car and offered to "take out" the individual with the weapon. I politely declined their offer, knowing that such an action would turn a violent riot into a gun battle since there was more than one weapon in the crowd. Instead, I told them that they were now under my direction and there were a number of essential tasks for them, the first being an attempt to establish communications with MND (SW) and SFOR Headquarters to apprise them of the current situation.[40] The JCOs cheerfully acquiesced and put themselves, and later their whole team, under my command for what eventually became almost a week. They were a great group of soldiers who provided me invaluable assistance in the days to come.[41]

Near mid-afternoon, with the worst of the violence subsiding, the new Commander of MND (SW), Major-General Cedric Delves, and a number of his staff, arrived by helicopter where I was located at W/H/153. Coincidently, he had taken command only that day and we had not previously met. Although, it was relatively calm in the immediate vicinity, the rioters had moved to the nearby downtown core of Drvar and continued the violence. I introduced myself as the on-site commander and provided a brief on the town's current situation. Delves, drawing on his previous experience in Northern Ireland, directed me to send soldiers downtown "to keep the crowd moving." I replied that given the low numbers of soldiers available, the current threats, and the necessity of protecting the Serbians, only a section of six to eight with their armour vehicle could be spared. Sending such a small number into a violent mob numbering in the hundreds "would be like throwing buns to an elephant."[42] I also continued that it would also create a situation where the soldiers would have to extricate themselves using lethal force, as the company had neither non-lethal means nor the permission to employ them if they did possess them. Delves once again directed that soldiers be sent to the area of the riot to force the mob to keep moving and I politely declined. A long pause ensured with both of us staring into each other's eyes. I then promised to send troops downtown once reinforcements arrived and a reasonable number, much greater than what was currently available, could be dispatched. After a few moments Delves reiterated his direction and departed for the Camp, to establish communications with the MND (SW) Headquarters.

Soon after this the BG Armour Squadron, C Squadron Royal Canadian Dragoons, arrived and commenced patrol operations. Within the hour another infantry company, Delta Company arrived at my location and was sent to the downtown area. There events unfolded as I suspected they would. Their armour vehicles were inundated by the crowd and in one case rammed by a civilian car. Warning shots were used to extricate themselves and the vehicles moved back to a position of observation near W/H/153 and remained disengaged.

The reaction of Delves to my non-compliance speaks volumes about the nature of command in multinational environments. Both of us recognized the character of that relationship and implicitly acknowledged it in defusing our potential confrontation. While given Delves' right to direct tactical operations of subordinate units regardless of nationality, I had an obligation to act in a manner commensurate with the intent of my BG and Canadian national authorities. The situation that could have been provoked by sending a small group into the riot could have invoked the ROE needlessly. There would have been much to lose and little to gain with such an action. I also realized at that time that even if Delves had chosen to relieve me of command there was no one to replace me within a reasonable period and unless I was physically removed, I was confident that my soldiers would continue to accept my direction. While there were no overt repercussions from this incident I can honestly say in the months that followed the Commander MND (SW) may have forgiven me but he did not forget. Our exchanges were unctuously correct but no more, contrasting with the familiarity he demonstrated towards other members of the BG.

Even though the A/CO, Major MacCallum and the BG Operations Officer, Major Joseph Shipley, had flown in by late afternoon and proceeded to the Camp to confer with Delves, the BG HQ had no functioning physical command and control capability in the area, which was compounded by the fact the MacCallum was assisting the Divisional Commander in negotiations with local Croatian officials and *hors d'combat*. Our direction was to "Keep doing what we were doing" and so we did. I asked all major elements in the area to agree to my command as the in-place commander and absorbed any others, regardless of nationality, into our ad hoc organization. Although very unwieldy, it worked until the BG assumed command of the Drvar area in the late evening. We were relieved by a British mechanized infantry company (A Company the Royal Greenjackets), at W/H/153 the next morning.[43]

During the following days Operation Wembley was initiated and led to an evacuation of the returnees at W/H/153 and increased security presence in Drvar for the next few months. With the removal of those Bosnian Serbians from the centre of town an uneasy peace settled and was maintained until the new contingent from the 3 RCR BG arrived in July.

After a great deal of introspection concerning the larger implications of the riot of 24 April and the surrounding events it seems as if the Croatians experienced a great deal of success in the short term but ultimately failed. At the immediate tactical level, while they achieved most of their destructive objectives they failed because they were unable to kill someone or cause the Canadians to exercise lethal force and create a Bosnian Croatian martyr. However, outweighing this was the larger immediate strategic success that the outcome of the riots produced for the Croatians. Their actions permitted them to delay further returns of Serbians for the immediate future and it attracted SACEUR's personal attention towards the local Croatian power structure. He eventually came several times to speak with the local Croatian officials and in keeping with the profile the area had attained the OHR appointed a special representative to coordinate events in Drvar.

Nonetheless, concomitant with this overwhelming high-level attention was a corresponding negative impact on SFORs field partners; the IOs, the PVOs, and the NGOs, who left Drvar as they felt that after the April riots SFOR could not protect them. There was an after action review, within 72 hours of the riots. It was chaired by the SACEUR, conducted by me, attended by Commander SFOR, General Eric Shinseki and many of the leaders of the IC.[44] It was the opinion of many of these agencies that they had not received enough protection during the violence. Some complained that lethal force should have been used for the protection of the field workers, regardless of level of danger that had been present. Others could not understand why deadly violence had not been used to protect the property and vehicles of these agencies.[45] Unfortunately, too late, it was realised that some of the misunderstanding between SFOR and the various humanitarian groups lay in different appreciations of the extent of military responsibilities and capabilities.

Nevertheless, without the humanitarian infrastructure to support them, the return of Serbians slowed to a trickle, and progress in the Drvar region was reduced to a standstill for the time being. Despite this, the rate of returns later recovered and the region is now almost completely in the hands of the original Serbian proprietors. For us who were there that day the most appropriate epithet did not originate from Canadian sources but was written by American military historian, Rick Swain, in *Neither War Nor Not War*. He opined that once the contingent in Drvar had realized they were "in a fight" they had "responded with skill and courage" and despite all that occurred they had "avoided disaster or the use of deadly force."[46]

EPILOGUE:

A Deputy Chief of the Defence Staff Commendation was awarded by Lieutenant-General R.R. Henault, on 23 August 1999, to the 1st Battalion, The Royal Canadian Regiment. It read:

> *In recognition of steadfast and professional action in the face of large scale civil unrest in the town of Drvar, Bosnia-Herzegovina on 24 April 1998. Soldiers of the 1 RCR Battle Group acted quickly and with great composure to place themselves between a violent crowd and unarmed refugees, preventing almost certain injuries and loss of life. Having acted with courage and restraint in resisting the temptation to shoot hostile belligerents, the Battle Group preserved the foundation for a restoration of peaceful relations between ethnic communities, bringing credit to themselves and to the Canadian Forces.[47]*

ENDNOTES

1   The credit for this story belongs to the men and women serving with and attached to the 1st Battalion Royal Canadian Regiment Battle Group (1RCR BG) during January to July 1998. Their daily courage and dedication were both inspirational and humbling. They taught me much and I will be forever in their debt.

2   Cited in Timothy Donais, "Peace without Prosperity: The Legacy of Peacebuilding in Drvar," *Peace Magazine* 20, No 3 (July/September 2004): 16 [internet] available at http://www.peacemagazine.org/archive/v20n3p16.htm, accessed 01 August 2005.

3   Cited in "Croatia's Serbs: Stormy Memories," *The Economist* 376, no. 8437 (July 30th – August 5th 2005): 45.

4   Figures taken from the International Crisis Group, "A Hollow Promise? Return of Bosnian Serb Displaced Persons to Drvar: Europe Report N°29," (19 January 1998), 3 [internet] available at http://www.crisisgroup.org/home/index.cfm?id=1576&l=1, accessed 02 August 2005.

5   The initial NATO military mission in support of the Dayton Accords was the Implementation Force (IFOR). IFOR was followed by SFOR once the original mandate to

support the disengagement of forces and stabilization of the region had occurred. This change signified the transition to a peace support operation that had many components, not just peace enforcement.

6   The General Framework Agreement for Peace in BH stated, "All refugees and displaced persons have the right freely to return to their homes of origin." Office of the High Representative and European Union Special Representative, Article I "Rights of Refugees and Displaced Persons" to Annex 7 "Agreement on Refugees and Displaced Persons" in the General Framework Agreement for Peace in Bosnia and Herzegovina (14 December 1995) [internet] available at http://www.ohr.int/, accessed 01 August 2005.

7   It was explained by 1 Guard's Brigade officers that *Ante Bruno Busic* was a Croatian author with nationalist leanings, who was killed for his work in 1978 at Paris. The Brigade was named after him to commemorate both his memory and the spirit of Croatian nationalism.

8   For information on Finvest and its involvement in Drvar see Alternativna Informativna Mreza (AIM), "Privileged Forest Buyers: The Rub is in Politics," (16 April 2001) [internet], available at http://www.aimpress.ch/dyn/trae/archive/data/200104/10416-002-trae-sar.htm, accessed 05 September 2005.

9   The term IC is utilized to represent a plethora of external western agencies that were involved in the region.

10   Canada, 1 RCR BG, *Keeping Peace & Freedom: Bosnia & Herzegovina January to July 1998* (1998), 3.

11   The leave plan required that each person was allocated a 21 day block of leave in addition to a couple of three day passes. It became quite a leadership challenge to manage this, while maintaining a functioning and well-led organization.

12   *Mir* means "peace" in Serbo-Croation.

13   "The position of High Representative was created under the General Framework Agreement for Peace in BiH (Dayton Peace Agreement) of 14 December 1995 to oversee implementation of the civilian aspects of the Peace Agreement. The mission of the High Representative (who is also the European Union's Special Representative) is to work with the people of BiH and the International Community to ensure that Bosnia and Herzegovina is a peaceful, viable state on course to European integration." *OHR* [internet] available at http://www.ohr.int/, accessed 05 September 2005; and, it was thought that having Bosnian Serbian officers in the local police force would assist with the establishment of a just and impartial rule of law in the region. However, like many such

proposals it proved very difficult to institute, with both sides advocating their own agendas.

14   A detailed discussion of these activities is contained in the International Crisis Group, "A Hollow Promise? Return of Bosnian Serb Displaced Persons to Drvar: Europe Report No. 29."

15   The Reconnaissance Squadron, commanded by Major John Schneidenbanger, had been re-rolled as an infantry company with two platoons of Strathcona's and one platoon from the Princess Patricia's Canadian Light Infantry. They had experienced some incidents protesting returns during fall 1997, including arson and small-scale mob violence. Major Schneidenbanger ensured that we were apprised of all details of those events.

16   The Battle Group was part of Multi-National Division South West (MND(SW)).

17   1 RCR BG, *Keeping Peace & Freedom*, 42.

18   These fieldworkers belong to Impact Teams International (ITI) a Hawaii-based religious organization that sent volunteers to various devastated regions of the world to alleviate suffering. They were affiliated with UNHCR in the Drvar area.

19   The SFOR Rules of Engagement (ROE) designated aid workers, amongst others, as Persons with Designated Special Status (PDSS). All measures up to and including Deadly Force were authorized to protect those who were PDSS. Canada, Department of National Defence, Canadian Contingent Stabilization Forces (CCSFOR) Rules of Engagement (ROE) Aide-Memoire For Commanders – Effective 22 January 1997.

20   Ibid., 44.

21   While I have reviewed this decision over the years, given the same hostility existed against all Serbian returnees both in and out of Drvar there was a need to continue patrolling day and night with the maximum manpower available. At that moment incidents were occurring throughout the area and I did not believe the threat level was any different for this couple than other isolated returnees. Despite this I have endured the personal consequences of that decision ever since. One can always intellectualize concerning the life and death choices military commanders may make and acknowledge that it is part of the profession; it is quite a different thing to experience the results and continue to command knowing that each daily operational directive, however well reasoned, may have disastrous consequences for the individuals involved. I can honestly say that after a six month tour in Drvar I, like many before me who have lived through similar times, changed in many ways.

22   As a result of their attempts to prevent the bodies from being destroyed, trying to extinguish the fire and most importantly ensuring there were no survivors left stranded Sergeant D.L. Paris, Master Corporal T.S. Turcotte, Privates S.T. Kelson, M.P. Stymiest and J.C.N. Weiss later received very much deserved Chief of Defence Staff Commendations for their sound judgment, coolness and courage.

23   The Commanding Officer, Lieutenant-Colonel Peter Devlin, had just returned to Canada for three weeks leave and to receive the Order of Military Merit from the Governor General for his record of outstanding service on behalf of Canada.

24   In order to obtain direct and unfiltered reports commanders sometimes utilize qualified and trusted officers to act as observers and report their findings. These special agents exist outside the chain of command and report back to the originating authority in the manner of a telescope directed towards a certain point. These officers provide feedback from specified units and operations. The JCOs acted in such a capacity within SFOR, reporting at that time to SFOR Headquarters in Sarajevo. The team that worked in Drvar was based on an American Special Forces team. The concept of the directed telescope is contained in Lieutenant-Colonel Gary B. Griffin, *The Directed Telescope: A Traditional Element of Effective Command* (Fort Leavenworth, KS: Combat Studies Institute, 1991), 1.

25   The Mortar Platoon consisted of members of the 2nd Regiment Royal Canadian Horse Artillery that had been seconded to the BG for OPERATION PALLADIUM. On 24 April this platoon consisted of less than 20 persons.

26   We used a variety of methods to do this, Motorola, telephone and physical contact by patrols.

27   One of the responsibilities of local fieldworkers within the different IC agencies was to keep their addresses up to date in the PDSS register at Camp Drvar. Despite the best efforts of the Company Second-in-Command, Captain Tom Mykytiuk, this had not been done. Needless to say after these events we did not experience the same difficulties in keeping that information current.

28   We maintained a standing QRF of one section (six to eight persons) on 15 minutes notice to move throughout the entire deployment. Given only nine sections were available for operations this was a significant but necessary task.

29   The CIMIC team consisting of Major Julio Dunich, Staff Sergeant Mike Hall and Lance Corporal Lynn Blanke did sterling work that day. They assisted a number of internationals in escaping the area and likely saved the life of the UNHCR fieldworker, who could not have gotten away without them. After their return to the Camp they pitched in with the numerous things that needed to be done, helping wherever they could. Their

knowledge of the returnees also permitted us to focus and prioritise protective activities over the following days.

30   A number of municipal work vehicles had been donated to the returned Bosnian Serbians. These consisted of a couple of fire trucks, a snowplough and two other utility vehicles. It was one of those fire trucks that had responded to the report of the fire in the centre of town. These vehicles were all destroyed later that day.

31   The ROE directed members of SFOR to intervene in instances where injury or death could be the outcome, regardless of who was involved.

32   The Mayor was later evacuated by helicopter and made a full recovery in the months that followed. I later found out that he had been attacked outside the town hall and rescued by a member of the Royal Canadian Mounted Police, Inspector Edward Josey, then stationed at the IC complex with the International Police Task Force. He had carried Marcetta as far as he could while being chased by angry Bosnian Croatians. Josey only left the bloodied body behind when he thought that Marcetta was dead and that he was now in danger of being killed for no good reason. He was later awarded the Meritorious Service Medal (Civil Division) for his efforts to save Marcetta.

33   Once all the internationals were accounted for these elements began to temporarily relocate isolated families into larger groups that would deter small scale harassment due to their increased size. We equipped them with flares to attract the attention of our patrols if they had need for assistance. Though some Croatians did eventually venture into the outlying areas that day no incidents occurred.

34   Captain Mykytiuk was in Canada on leave.

35   Several rounds had been fired by two soldiers who had been isolated by the mob during their attempt to rejoin the Mortar Platoon; two other sets of warning shots had been fired in an attempt to discourage the crowd from occupying the school house. In all there were six incidents of warning shots that day. 1 RCR 3350-1 (OC C Coy) *RECORD OF WARNING SHOTS – DRVAR RIOT 24 APR 98* dated 28 Apr 98.

36   Delta Company, another infantry company in the 1 RCR BG, had been occupying W/H/153 since the murders and departed that morning. WO Laidlaw and his staff were acting in the capacity of rear party, ensuring that all remaining stores and equipment were packed and transported. The two British dog handlers and their dogs were attached from MND (SW) to assist with security patrols in town, in the same manner as police dogs. Unfortunately, one of the dog handlers had succumbed to some form of combat stress, was completely non-communicative and his dog would not let anyone close to him. We later found out that he was a new soldier recently graduated from basic trade training. Due to

the shortage of specialists he was almost immediately sent on a deployment, without normal employment time and integration in the United Kingdom. For this inexperienced soldier the results of this rushed deployment were dire.

37   We had no portable barriers or readily accessible barbed wire. This deficiency was later remedied.

38   Sam, the German Shepard, was later awarded the Dickin Medal, for his efforts in Drvar. BBC, "War medal given to hero dog," (20 December 2002) [internet], available at http://news.bbc.co.uk/1/hi/england/2593963.stm, accessed 05 September 2005.

39   This helicopter was one of two that had been stationed at the Camp; as soon as they could they readied themselves for flight and operated continuously for the rest of the day. I found their reports invaluable, as they could accurately see and report the movement of the crowds surrounding us and within the town. This permitted me to efficiently deploy and redeploy the limited troops available to neutralize threats.

40   The JCOs were equipped with portable satellite telephones could place calls anywhere in the world.

41   Due to their mandate they were not bound by the same strictures as us and they gathered an enormous amount of tactical information on our behalf.

42   This expression is attributable to Captain David Ellis, a fellow platoon commander in Golf Company, 2RCR when I was newly commissioned in the 1980s.

43   Coincidentally, I had met the British Company Commander in passing on a previous tour with the United Nations Protection Force in Croatia during 1994. He had been serving on exchange as a Company Second-in-Command with 1 PPCLI. The relief-in-place had been arranged by MND (SW) and this company was equipped with non-lethal weapons systems and protective equipment.

44   Within a day General Shinseki had arrived at Drvar, conducted his own review of what had taken place and told us he was satisfied with our actions. He visited the soldiers in the camp and all who came in contact with him were impressed with his warmth and presence.

45   Amongst the detractors was the UN Special Envoy Jacques Kline, who had been directly blaming the BG for the degree of destruction that took place during the riot. Although he was not at the After Action Review, which supported our actions, he continued to degenerate the role that had been played by the Canadians. Eventually, General Shinseki intervened and made him desist. Kline later penned an apology to the BG.

46   Richard M. Swain, *Neither War Nor Not War Army Command in Europe During the Time of Peace Operations: Tasks Confronting USAREUR Commanders, 1994-2000* (Carlisle, Pennsylvania: United States Army War College, Strategic Studies Institute, May 2003): 17.

47   *Honours and Awards as a result of the riots of 24 April 1998*: Major Greg MacCallum – The Royal Canadian Regiment; Acting Commanding Officer *Queen's Decoration for Valuable Service (United Kingdom)*; Captain Brian Bedard – Royal Canadian Artillery Mortar Platoon Commander, *Mention in Dispatches (MID) (United Kingdom)*; Master Warrant Officer Derek Ingersoll – The Royal Canadian Regiment Charles Company Sergeant Major *MID (United Kingdom)*; Warrant Officer George Laidlaw – The Royal Canadian Regiment, Delta Company Quartermaster Sergeant, *Chief of Defence Staff Commendation (Canada)*; Major Julio Dunich – United States Army Reserve, Commander Civil Military Cooperation Team, *Soldier's Medal (United States)* Staff Sergeant Mike Hall – United States Marine Corps Reserve Civil Military Cooperation Team, *Joint Commendation Medal (United States)*; Lance Corporal Lynn Blanke Civil Military Cooperation Team, *Defense Meritorious Service Medal (United States)*; Charles Company –1st Battalion, The Royal Canadian Regiment, *Canadian Contingent Stabilization Force Commander's Citation*; Delta Company – 1st Battalion, The Royal Canadian Regiment, *Canadian Contingent Stabilization Force Commander's Citation*; Mortar Platoon – 2nd Regiment, Royal Canadian Horse Artillery, *Canadian Contingent Stabilization Force Commander's Citation*. The individual and collective military awards were administered by a variety of organizations, reflected in this list and is completed to my best knowledge. Other awards may have been presented in connection with this incident but are unknown to me.

CHAPTER 6

OPERATION CENTRAL: PERSPECTIVES OF THE OFFICER COMMANDING THE DISASTER ASSISTANCE RESPONSE TEAM (DART) COMPANY

Lieutenant-Colonel Ian C. MacVicar

I was employed as Battery Commander, "E" Battery, in the 2nd Regiment, The Royal Canadian Horse Artillery (2 RCHA) during a very busy fall training campaign in 1998. I had spent most of September and October in the field "sleeping rough" almost every night with my Artillery Forward Observation tactical groups in weather ranging from a beautiful "Indian Summer" days through torrential rain to freezing sleet. My artillery observation teams' lives had mirrored those of our infantry colleagues in the 1st Battalion, The Royal Canadian Regiment (1 RCR) during this period as we lived from either our armoured personnel carriers (APCs) or our trenches for weeks at a time. Individual Ration Packs, (occasionally even heated) were the usual daily menu. All in all, it was an excellent preparation for the physical and mental challenges that followed during Operation Central in November and December of that year.

On Sunday night, 1 November 1998, I had just returned from the Militia Training Centre (MTC) Meaford where I had been employed as the coordinator of the tactical evaluation of the 49th Field Regiment, Royal Canadian Artillery (RCA) of Sault Ste. Marie. On Monday morning, 2 November, I received a phone call from Lieutenant-Colonel Wayne Douglas of the 1st Canadian Division Headquarters in Kingston, who held the secondary duty of Commanding Officer of the yet untried Disaster Assistance Response Team (DART). I held the secondary duty of Company Commander of the yet untried DART Company. Ironically, I had been advised by the previous holder of this duty that it had been a boring and unfulfilling exercise in stock taking and measuring readiness across 2 Canadian Mechanized Brigade Group (CMBG) units with a constantly changing cast of characters. That was to change in late October 1998, after Hurricane MITCH swept through the Caribbean Sea, leaving behind an estimated 10,000 dead and hundreds of thousands homeless.

THE DART MISSION.

Initial Deployment. Prior to our departure Lieutenant-Colonel Douglas passed me an unofficial warning order and an update by telephone on 2 and 3 November 1998 respectively. He advised me that he had not yet received his official orders but that he had to depart soon on the strategic reconnaissance and wanted to facilitate the maximum time available for battle procedure. Given the shortened time available I requested permission to call the DART members together from 2 CMBG headquarters (HQ), which was granted on or about 3 November for action the next day.

I gathered the DART primary and alternate leaders together in the 2 RCHA lecture theatre on 4 November and briefed them on their probable mission and advised them to begin their administrative preparations for departure. Although all the DART primary and alternate members had supposedly been through all of these preparations we nonetheless found that there were significant gaps in the numbers of fully prepared personnel. I personally went through a quick round of inoculations, updated my will, received a new passport, and was interviewed by the local CTV affiliate regarding the mission. Given my own "newness" to the DART Company I relied heavily on the prepared media response lines from National Defence Headquarters (NDHQ). I did, however, comment in complete honesty that I felt that the 2 CMBG troops were up to whatever tasks lay ahead given the hectic Fall training schedule and the recent deployment to Bosnia that many had been through within the last six months. These troops were well prepared to face adverse conditions posed by either the physical or mission environments.

Lieutenant-Colonel Douglas led the strategic reconnaissance from 4-6 November, which selected the port of entry (POE), the Canadian Task Force Headquarters, the supply base, and defined the general Area of Operations for Operation Central. After organizing the Departure Assistance Group (DAG) through 2 CMBG HQ, I departed for 8 Wing/CFB Trenton on 5 November where we underwent a second DAG.

The four member tactical reconnaissance team departed Trenton at 0100 hours 6 November 1998, stuffed in the back of a CC-130 Hercules transport aircraft. Seating was extremely limited and the Company Sergeant-Major (CSM) and I sacked out on the canvass top of the Light

Support Vehicle Wheel (LSVW) trailer. After a rather uneventful five-hour trip we landed at McDill Air Force Base (AFB) in Florida, where we observed USAF troops conducting Physical Training at 0600 hours to avoid the already noticeable heat. We left McDill AFB approximately two hours later, en route to La Ceiba, the Canadian POE on the Atlantic coast of Honduras.

On arrival in La Ceiba, Honduras, Lieutenant-Colonel Douglas met the tactical reconnaissance team, which I led, and included the CSM, Master Warrant Officer Nelson Lizotte, and a Reconnaissance (recce) Sergeant from the 2nd Combat Engineer Regiment (2 CER) and a sergeant from the 2 Military Police (MP) Platoon.

Helicopter Over Flight of the Aguan Valley. As the bridge over the Rio Cangrejal and the main road arteries had been swept away by the massive floods we resorted to helicopter over flights to gain an appreciation of the hurricane's impact. We took off from La Ceiba in a Griffon helicopter of 427 Tactical Helicopter Squadron of Petawawa. We landed seven or eight times across the Valley to assess the degree of destruction through observation and discussion with the local inhabitants. Aside from being hungry, many of the people were wearing rags and had numerous skin maladies. In one village almost all the people appeared to have a "pink eye" type of mange from head to foot!

As for the physical damage, my initial impression was that if you compared the green jungle foliage to a carpet, then someone had reached down and rolled the carpet back from the coast to the Valley, revealing the brown underlay. The brown "carpet" underlay resembled the photographs I had seen of the destruction of the first Atomic Bombs at Hiroshima and Nagasaki. There seemed to be absolutely nothing left! Highway bridges were scattered like "Lego" toys. Thousands of vehicles and houses were buried. We saw hundreds of dead animals. Initially we had digitally marked their positions for later disposal with the Griffon Helicopter Global Positioning System (GPS), however, as the flight wore on it became obvious that the disposal task was going to be beyond our capabilities.

The second major impression that stuck with me was the smell – the sickly sweet smell of death was everywhere. Below 1000 feet Above Ground Level (AGL) you started to notice it. At one point we were descending to the village of La Cuveee des Islettas, when Dan Etheridge, the Engineer Recce Troop sergeant, leaned over and asked, "Do you smell that?" We both knew without any discussion what it was. When we landed the villagers pointed out that there were "seven people buried in that collapsed structure under the mud" or "there's four in here," and so on. While the smell was quite evident, we did not actually see individual fatal casualties. They appeared to be buried and beyond hope.

This gave me some pause for thought as I had expected that we were in a race against time to rescue casualties prior to their deaths from the initial effects of the flooding and collapse of structures. In fact, the initial killing wave had done its work by the time we arrived a week later. I realized that our main challenge would be to prevent the spread of secondary effects of water borne diseases such as typhoid, cholera, and malaria. There was also the unexpected, but occasional fights for the remaining food and shelter among the surviving populace – which led to the occasional gunshot and machete wounds that we treated. Indeed, our first casualty was a young woman with a gunshot wound to her lower body. She had been shot in a struggle with a neighbor over a chicken. Needless to say the chicken lost regardless of the outcome!

Our final stop was the village of Sonaguera, where we examined two potential DART campsites. I selected the local Dole Fruit factory compound on the outskirts of Sonaguera, as it was along the Main Supply Route, and was also fenced, level, relatively dry, and had water holding tanks. The alternate site, the local soccer field in the village, only met the criterion for size – it was deficient in all other areas.

After examining the 1000 square kilometer area of operational responsibility, Lieutenant-Colonel Douglas's direction was brief and to the point. He was going to return to La Ceiba to coordinate the strategic aspects of the mission. I had his full support in whatever operational and tactical level plans I devised "to sort it out". I saw him twice over the next five weeks but did manage to have at least one weekly telephone call when the satellite reception permitted it.

Passage of Mission Information. I passed the initial warning order to the DART primary and alternate personnel at the 2 RCHA lecture theatre in CFB Petawawa. They then conducted internal orders groups within their own units. Once in theatre I drafted the initial deployment orders with the J4 staff of the Joint Task Force headquarters – Central America

(JTF-CAM) to move the DART Company from the POE at La Ceiba to Sonaguera in the Aguan Valley

After arrival the arrival of the first DART main body group on 9 November I passed information through two means:

    a.   a morning coordination conference that included Honduran and multinational aid agency representatives; and

    b.   an evening DART Company orders group that confirmed tasks for the next day. These orders groups were followed by orders at platoon and section level.

Ensuring Commitment and Mission Success. After the arrival of the last packet of the DART main body in Sonaguera, I spoke to the assembled DART Company members describing my initial recce and how the sick, injured, and displaced Hondurans could be your family member in different circumstances. While I do not believe that this message affected all DART members I could tell that it struck many as appropriate by the looks on their faces as they listened. I later reinforced that the mission was important, right in scope and supported by both the Canadian people and our CF comrades.

HOW TO BUILD AN EFFECTIVE TEAM.

I believed that I could appeal to the basic human instinct of wanting to help other people in distress. By and large this concept worked although I did have to emphasize on several occasions that the cynical point of view that we were only in Honduras to earn domestic and international political points was only a side effect of the real good we were doing for real people in distress.

How Diverse was the Unit? The Dart Company was incredibly diverse:

    a.   Headquarters Platoon was comprised of soldiers from across 2 RCHA, including Signals Branch personnel with significant experience on foreign deployments;

    b.   The Defence & Security Platoon was comprised almost entirely of soldiers from "E" Battery, 2 RCHA. Most of these troops had been in the field for ten months (including a tour in Bosnia, the Fall training campaign and now the deployment on Op Central. There was an obvious difference in how tightly knit they were in comparison with the other contributing units;

c.   Medical Platoon was based on soldiers from 2 Field Ambulance, with augmentation from across the CF;

d.   Engineer Troop, was based on 2 CER;

e.   Logistics Platoon was comprised mainly of troops from 2 Service Battalion; and

f.   Short notice technical trade augmentees came from across the CF, e.g. Water, Fuel and Environmental Techs (WFE), Plumber Gas Fitters from CFBs Cold Lake and Trenton, and a Preventive Medical Technician Warrant Officer from Defence and Civil Institute of Environmental Medicine (DCIEM) Toronto.

Team Change During Mission. There was relatively little change to the basic DART Company establishment during the five and a half week deployment although there was a constant small trickle of people "left out of battle" due to illnesses acquired in the tropical environment and the odd injury. As the task grew in scope there was some movement of specialized trades from JTF-CAM HQ in La Ceiba to augment the deployed DART Company at Sonaguera. For example, we stood up a Military Police section to assist in traffic control and route marking in the Aguan Valley; and to work with the local authorities in crime prevention. As we were sitting on large quantities of food and drugs there was also the possibility of theft from either the base camp or from deployed DART elements.

The command structure was changed half way through the mission due to several factors not forecast in the original DART concept. Due to the larger CF contingent the designated DART commanding officer (CO), Lieutenant-Colonel Douglas, was appointed Commander JTF-Central American (JTF-CAM) and each of the subordinate element commanders were designated as commanding officers to permit greater autonomy in dealing with disciplinary and administrative issues.

Needless to say, due to the three hour distance and poor communications between the JTF-CAM HQ in La Ceiba and the DART Company at Sonaguera this upgrading of my authority was well received. DART company tasks were almost entirely self generated in accordance with my own priority of effort based on observations made by the troops during their missions, the input from local authorities, non-governmental organizations, and my own weighing of the "troops to tasks." I had several cases where I used my authority as a CO to resolve disciplinary issues. No charges were laid under the National Defence Act (NDA) but several administrative procedures were actioned.

Techniques in Team Building. New team members were given a couple of days to acclimatize prior to being sent on missions in the jungle or mountains. There were always integrated with personnel that had been in theatre since the start of the mission.

Given that the last packet of the main body arrived on 11 November, I held a Remembrance Day parade where I made references to past Canadian sacrifices during wartime and recent peace support missions. As CFB Petawawa had suffered a number of losses in Bosnia over the last few years it was not difficult to draw analogies to the nature of sacrifice in military duty. I also enlisted the help of the Police Chief of Sonaguera and local clergy in the ceremony, which certainly made it a unique service in comparison to our usual parades in Canada. The presence of the Honduran citizens lent the service a certain dignity as they had not only suffered recent losses through Hurricane MITCH, but had also suffered losses and displacement during their civil war in the late 1970s/early 1980s. Interestingly, Sonaguera means "Sound of War".

I also researched the history of the long established Gunner custom of handing parades over "At Ease" in recognition of hard labour. The Adjutant 2 RCHA sent me the requisite pages from the Standing Orders for The Royal Regiment of Canadian Artillery through the mail. I explained this custom to the troops on a company parade held after about two weeks in country, and told them that I believed that they deserved the same recognition as the Artillery given the hours they were working. Given that the backbone of the DART Company were from 2 RCHA this was not a difficult transition.

In addition, all plans were discussed to assess the pros and cons within the daily morning coordination conferences and once decided, issued as orders at the nightly "O Groups". This not only ensured the best possible plans would be devised, but it also gave individuals a feeling of inclusion.

We also held a "name the camp" contest with the winner getting time off in La Ceiba. The winning entry was "Camp Ayuda," which means "assistance" in Spanish.

Although I gave many (24) interviews, I tried to focus the numerous Canadian and foreign media on talking to the troops about their roles and how it supported the overall DART mission. This worked well with troops who were proud of their role and personal contribution.

The canteen and CF Personnel Support Agency (PSA) movies helped with morale. These were established during the second week of operations. The authorization of a wet canteen after week 3 also helped to raise spirits. In addition, we had various fund-raising events to buy food for the displaced Honduran populace. The 158 of us raised approximately $2000.00 in this effort. We even had several people shave their heads for charity. I went as far as to shave my moustache for money. Once people donated their money to the mission they could be said to have well and truly "bought into it"!

Another important aspect was Padre (Captain) Kelly Bokovay's weekly divine services, including some with the local Honduran clergy. He was always available to meet with any DART member under stress. Moreover, a family support telephone through one of the satellite phones was authorized after about three weeks.

How to Handle Non-Team Players. Given the wide number of trades represented within the DART Company, I knew that we could not treat everyone as if they were combat arms soldiers who were accustomed to strong internal discipline and set teams. A different approach was required. As such, we would draw out their individual skills with the assistance of their internal chains of command and try to apply them as soon as possible. Once they saw the value of their work this problem usually disappeared.

The Padre was worth his weight in gold. As some of our non-combat arms personnel appeared to be under more stress due to the climatic extremes and long hours, I made a joke of telling them that if the Padre could handle it so could they. Captain Bokovay, an ex-infantry captain, former pioneer platoon commander, and qualified parachutist was in on the joke and kept his service background hidden as best he could. This little leadership "scam" was eventually discovered by the troops who let me know that they were impressed by the toughness of the Padre and also by the subterfuge of their OC and later CO.

Building Confidence. Success bred success. Once the DART personnel saw the results of their work in the displaced communities their self-confidence was reinforced. This generally extended to the overall mission although the cynical comment of being a giant "photo op" did crop up from time to time.

MISSION CHANGE

The DART concept was relatively static. I realized that the people isolated in the mountain villages and cut off by the flood waters were not going to make their way to our base camp for aid or food. Therefore, I recommended that the helicopter assets be integrated within the Company's daily operations as our means of transport for the medical, engineer, and water supply teams. This would allow greater reach. Once the coordination was effected with JTF-CAM HQ, this heliborne deployment concept worked well.

ETHICAL DILEMMAS.

At times an aid agency or a township/village leader would try to influence the delivery and timing of aid resources. In such circumstances right/wrong could become blurred as they pled their case. Exaggerations of the degree of need and number of proportionate casualties were not uncommon. I always kept it simple – what action would bring the greatest good for the greatest number of people with the least risk of mission failure or loss of CF personnel. For example, one night a Mormon missionary requested a special night helicopter medical evacuation of a woman dying of advanced Tuberculosis in a remote mountain village. I refused citing the risk to the crew and the fact that her children would be left with no support if she died at the hospital in Tegucigalpa. I was later advised this was the best decision under the circumstances as there were other relatives available to take care of her children in her village.

IN HARM'S WAY.

Although a humanitarian mission, there were elements of danger, and although this only occurred in a few isolated instances such as fording the Rio (river) Cangrejal outside La Ceiba, and when shots were fired in the vicinity of the camp by local criminals trying to provoke a response or gauge the reaction time of our Defence & Security Reaction Force, it was always a serious consideration. I realized that it was important to recognize fear in others (e.g. speaking rapidly, fidgeting, zoning out at inappropriate times) so that a timely response could be made – such as reassurances, personal example or simply explaining the situation in greater detail.

In addition there was an ever present danger of criminal, particularly narco-trafficker activity. There was an initial lack of Rules of Engagement (ROE) in what was presumed to be a benign environment. While there were no belligerents in theatre, there were lots of drug runners and several threats against the camp. The manager of the Dole Fruit Company factory, Senor Arturo Fortin, had a friend killed in a bar over extortion schemes. There was a contract on Senor Fortin's head, leading him to carry a pistol all the time. After our arrival, the Police Chief of Sonaguera immediately offered the unit protection through a loan of weapons and or members of his force. Given the heavy drug industry presence in the area I immediately petitioned NDHQ for defensive ROEs, which were granted within three days.

Overall, we had very few stress casualties – those that we had appeared to be short in nature. They seemed more related to being overwhelmed by the scope of the disaster and the sad outcome of some individual cases. Talking the issues through with peers or the Padre seemed to alleviate this problem. "Black humour" helped in a few of the sad cases that we could not help, although this was done in a very circumspect manner.

We also suffered only a few minor CF casualties from traffic accidents, insect bites, and tropical illnesses. Personnel requiring serious attention were evacuated by helicopter to La Ceiba and the JTF-CAM HQ medical section. Nonetheless, we witnessed thousands of Honduran nationals with afflictions ranging from gunshot and machete wounds to broken limbs, dehydration, and serious pre-existing health problems that had worsened since the flood. I believe that there was a natural barrier that prevented our personnel from becoming too personally involved with the Honduran patients. This was more difficult when the patients were children.

To ensure our mental and physical health, most of the troops followed unit directed physical fitness programs, some of which were quite intensive. However, the soldiers were in fact best helped by their pre-deployment fitness training – not during the deployment. The 12-14 hour work days, the tropical extremes of heat and rain, and the threat of extortion and kidnapping from narco-traffickers, led to my instituting a policy whereby PT was conducted within the confines of our camp or in large groups outside the wire. I did not permit individual PT; nor "walking out" privileges outside our compound other than on Saturday mornings.

In addition, we followed a very strict discipline regarding local food and water. In short we didn't drink it! In addition, all members were inoculated against various tropical diseases and we took Doxycycline, a broad spectrum anti-biotic daily. Doxycycline was reputed to be 98 percent effective against Vivax malaria. Unfortunately doxycycline failed in approximately 15 percent of the cases, including in mine.

On average the troops worked a 12 hour day compared to the HQ and operations staff who worked a 12 to 15 hour day. We did allow one half day off per week for each member to relax, sleep, or try to clean their clothes. In addition, we had one sports day on 6 December 1998, to celebrate Christmas and Saint Barbara's Day for the Gunners and Engineers. We had a soccer game with a local Sonaguera team, which graciously won by only one goal!

CULTURAL ISSUES

The Honduran concept of time versus the Canadian concept of time was very flexible. When I briefed the Honduran medical authorities that the CF helicopters would depart at 0730 hours, the helicopters were ready depart at 0730 hours! However, it was not uncommon for the medical authhorities to arrive for meetings up to an hour after the announced time. This misunderstanding cleared itself up within a few days once they realized that they could miss a helicopter ride. Following this realization on their part I was often asked, "Is that in Honduran time or Canadian time?"

CONCLUSION

In sum, commanding the DART Company was a challenging and rewarding experience. As always, the courage, tenacity and capability of Canada's service personnel were inspiring. Although the DART Company was largely an ad hoc organization, the training and experience of our soldiers, as well as their initiative, leadership capability and motivation to help others, allowed us to quickly forge a cohesive team. I hope the experiences and advice proffered in this chapter assist others who may find themselves in similar circumstances.

CHAPTER 7

CP-140 JOINS THE FIGHT:
THE DEPLOYMENT OF THE LONG RANGE
PATROL DETACHMENT –
OPERATION APOLLO, ROTO 0

Major Neil Tabbenor

As an Aerospace Engineer (AERE) I have spent my entire career to this point in the service of the CP-140 Long Range Patrol (LRP) aircraft, as a software engineer, a project manager, a first line maintenance officer, and now as the System Engineering Officer in the Director General AEPM. Without reservation, the highlight of my career in the Air Force has been my participation in Rotation (Roto) 0 of the LRP Detachment of Operation (Op) Apollo.

I believe that a serving member can spend their entire career without doing the job they are paid to do, that is the defence of Canada, an allied country, or coalition partner. That is especially true in some components of the Air Force, where real-world operations are few and far between. As such, from a personal perspective, Op Apollo was my opportunity to earn my pay.

In this endeavour, I saw people perform miracles. From the "Loggies," whom I hold in high regard, to the aircrews, to the technicians, who, like Scotty of Star Trek, overcame insurmountable odds to make broken aircraft serviceable. In utter disregard for the fact that we were all "blue-suiters," and not army guys with three rows of blue and white ribbons on their tunics, everyone came together in support of the mission in ways I never thought possible. Conversely, there were several occasions where severe head shaking was required, although that was normally caused by headquarters.

In the end, despite our inexperience, the inadequate preparation, and the conditions upon arrival, the deployment was an unqualified success. Within four days of main-body arrival we were launching missions.[1] Nearly 180 launches later, our Roto was ready to come home.

IN THE BEGINNING

After the unconscionable events of 11 September 2001 (9/11), when terrorists destroyed the twin towers of the World Trade Centre in New York, the rumours began to seriously circulate through 14 Wing, Greenwood. Supposedly, the United States Navy (USN) was looking to Canada to provide relief to allow its own LRP assets to engage in Operation Enduring Freedom. But like any good rumour, it had some basis in fact. Whether those rumours initiated the eventual deployment, like the tail wagging the dog, is still a mystery.

For those unfamiliar with the CP-140 Aurora, it is a multi mission reconnaissance and antisubmarine warfare aircraft manufactured by Lockheed Martin. It is based on the airframe of the United States Navy (USN) P 3C and the avionics of the S-3A Viking aircraft. Powered by four T56 turboprop engines, it is capable of ranges over 4000 nautical miles and speeds up to 405 knots (indicated airspeed).[2] Most mission profiles call for the Aurora to fly at 200 feet above water with No. 1 engine loitered, day or night. It is a truly remarkable and rugged piece of kit. Even today, my favourite part of an air show is the CP-140 high-speed fly past. The minimum crew consists of two pilots, one flight engineer, a tactical navigator (TACNAV), a navigator/communicator (NAVCOM), two acoustic sensor operators (ASO), and three non-acoustic sensor operators (NASO).[3] The ideal crew is 14; the remaining four are training positions.

When the announcement came on 1 October 2001, it was met with incredulity. Speculation on where, when, and for what purpose ran wild. The LRP community, at the time, was wholly unprepared for this kind of deployment. Certainly the CP-140 aircraft routinely deployed, but almost entirely to known, friendly, and supportive locations. Even then, deployments were limited to only a few weeks at a time.[4] At the very least, we had never deployed while using words like tent, pallet, pick handle, chock, mechanized shelter, Table of Organization &Equipment (TO&E), and Theatre Specific Mission Training (TSMT).

Within days the leadership positions had been selected, Lieutenant-Colonel (now Colonel) John Mitchell, then Commanding Officer (CO) of 405 Squadron (sqn), would lead the deployment. The operations, logistics, and maintenance flight commanders were Major Shawn Marley, Major

Dan Dorrington, and myself respectively. Chief Warrant Officer Jean-Guy Trudel was selected as the Detachment Warrant Officer.

There ensued some debate as whether I was the right choice for maintenance flight commander. Not that I was not up for it, I had the most CP-140 time and deployment experience of any AERE officer available. The problem was one of rank. At the time I was a captain, and therefore one half stripe short of equivalency. In hindsight, those who thought the job should have been given to a major had a point. Later I will discuss how the "camp" grew in size and responsibility. It was in an environment where the rank of major would have served me well. When dealing with the other two flight commanders, and certainly the boss, rank was never an issue. Not surprisingly, I vehemently disagreed with the argument that someone other than me should go. In the end, I won out, though I do not know if it was the logic of it or my desperate pleading that did the trick.

The Chief of the Air Staff Planning Guidance requires that a vanguard of two CP-140 Auroras be ready to deploy on 21 day's notice. Given our complete ignorance of vanguard level deployments, 21 days seemed all too short. The logistics guys came on board and helped lay out the plan; fill out the TO&E, order the airlift, conduct a combined strategic and tactical reconnaissance, train and "DAG" the personnel, pack the kit, arrange the "VIP" send off, and then we were gone.[5]

It was a difficult task about to become more so. We had no idea where we would be going, or what exactly we would be doing there. The CP-140 serves different mission roles, each with their own support requirements. Each passing day without a destination crowded the 21-day deadline without reprieve. The 21-day plan became the 14-day plan, and then, if you can fathom it, the seven-day plan. What started as unfeasible became impossible.

In the meantime, the personnel had to be chosen. Fortunately for me, I had two teams selected and prepped to participate in an upcoming short-deployment to Kinloss, Scotland. The third team was hand–picked from the remaining technicians. The operations flight had a more difficult time assembling qualified aircrews, but I will leave that story for someone else to tell. Later, near Christmas, higher headquarters (HQ) opened the operation to 407 Sqn (19 Wing), our sister unit on the West Coast. That meant the inclusion one of their aircrews and one of their maintenance teams. Easily, the most contentious decision of the entire deployment I had to make was which of the 14 Wing maintenance teams to cut to accommodate the 407 Sqn crew. This leads me to my first apology.

Early on I had assumed that upon being given notice of deployment, old war wounds would reappear, that non-negotiable family matters would suddenly manifest themselves, and that the printers would hum with release paperwork. I could not have been more wrong. Everyone wanted in. Others, not selected to deploy, repeatedly approached me asking to find them a place. I will reiterate, we did not know where we were going. By all rights we could have ended up living under green canvass in Coldbekistan for six months. And yet, everyone wanted to go. For my lack of trust in my technicians I apologise. Despite the unknowns and the tension, morale was astonishingly high.

The makeup of the maintenance flight was small and uncomplicated. It included myself; a Flight Warrant Officer, Master Warrant Officer (now Chief Warrant Officer) Jim Jardine; three crew chiefs, Sergeant Bowser Sawler, Sergeant Bruce Harkness, and Sergeant Renaud Moreau (all three are now warrant officers); three teams (crews) of 10 technicians, two photograph technicians, two support technicians, and six technicians to supplement the armament load crews.[6] I was receiving some pressure from my squadron to take more technicians - the conventional thinking being that more is better. I was worried, however, that we would end up living on a rock with nothing to do but the job and countered with the argument that I did not need guys bored and in search of their own entertainment, as this inevitably leads to unnecessary paperwork and charge parades. Later I will explain why that decision was wrong and issue a second apology.[7]

Nonetheless, to accommodate the crew from 19 Wing I cut the third team by process of elimination. "A" and "B" were given the go, "C" remained behind. The third Crew Chief became Sergeant (now Warrant Officer) Camil Guerin.[8] Thoughtlessly, I had neglected to check for any perceived conflicts of interest. My flight warrant officer was recently of "A" Crew, so members of "C" Crew took the decision personally, the implication being favouritism. I tried to explain the haphazard process by which I came to my decision to no avail. I explained that I would not purposely cut a leader as capable as Sergeant Moreau. They were not convinced. There are hard feelings over that issue to this day despite the fact that most of the "C"

Crew members deployed with later rotations (roto). Sadly for Sergeant Moreau, he suffered a terrible motorcycle accident just prior to his scheduled departure on Roto 1 and never had the opportunity to deploy on Op Apollo.

By the end of October the 21 days had passed without movement. Go here, stay there, on again - off again, turned days into weeks. What was to be (ostensibly) a six-month deployment eventually became nine. To a person, everyone who deployed on Roto 0 believed the first three months before actually deploying to be the most difficult. I distinctly recall one Friday receiving the word from HQ to move on the following Monday. The detachment commander and the other flight commanders were out on a combined strategic and tactical recce (several possible destinations were still under consideration), leaving me in charge of the detachment.[9] The sense of urgency by our higher HQ was overwhelming, though the reason for it escaped us. Anyone who has done any kind of planning knows how hard it is to do it right even in the best of circumstances. Having no destination (and for that matter, no mission definition) means uncertainty over the equipment, personnel, and airlift required.

Nevertheless, the remaining staff pulled an all-nighter to piece together a deployment plan. It went something like this: stuff the two CP-140s with as many people, parts, and kit as humanly possible. Fly to our "destination", live under the wings and dupe Bedouins into sparing us some gas.[10] I presented it to the Wing Commander the following day with every expectation that he would "tear me a new one." He took the "plan" seriously and was merciful, for which I am grateful. The Monday deployment did not happen, as if there was any doubt.

The remainder of the week was more of the same. Morale had crashed and the troops were becoming increasingly edgy with the uncertainty. Families suffered; they were weary of the constant yanking back and forth, and so was I. Although I was in charge, my rank paralleled most of the aircrew, and I under-ranked some. During the time the boss was away a few grew vocal about their discontent; threats were uttered. By the following Friday afternoon I began to believe we would get some respite. I even considered going to the mess for a beer. However, while leaving the Detachment HQ I was approached by Captain Denis Pleau, the acting logistics flight commander. He had just come from the Operations Room. The game was back on. Mercifully, this round was not allowed to progress as far as the first.

If I might make a personal observation, what could possibly be the point of conducting simultaneous recces? Their aims are exclusive of each other. My limited understanding of the subject tells me the strategic recce determines the best location from which to conduct the operation and initiates diplomatic contact. The tactical recce is then used to determine how to make that location viable. To do both together satisfied the urgency at the expense of efficacy. It was later speculated that the reason for the immediacy was we would soon be vying for airlift with the infantry battle group headed for Afghanistan.

The boss returned the following week. I shook his hand, welcomed the sight of him and informed him that he owed me many beers.[11] He brought good news; we knew where but not when.

The United Arab Emirates (UAE) is not Coldbekistan, quite the contrary. Parts of the UAE are very westernized and appear liberal when compared to the other Gulf States. It hardly resembles a country but is more a federation of seven Emirates, remnants of a tribal system, each ruled independently but represented by a single president, who is elected by the ruling elite of the Emirates. The political landscape of the UAE has remained essentially unchanged since 1972, when they became independent from the United Kingdom (UK). To my knowledge, they have very little by way of an equalization program as we do in Canada. The rich Emirates are extremely so, the poorer ones not so much. Abu Dhabi, the richest of the Emirates gains its wealth from oil. Dubai, the next in line, strives to be the banking and commercial sector of the Middle East. The other Emirates made do (as far as we could tell) by engaging in activities that should only be discussed with your Intelligence folks. The skyline of Dubai city is filled with incredible architecture. It boasts the famed Burg al Arab, better known as the sail hotel. With a seven star rating, it is unreservedly the world's most opulent. Unfortunately, a large portion of the office towers appeared unoccupied, displaying "To Let" signs. Their city planning seemed based on a policy of "build it and they will come". It was Dubai that we were to call home.

As December 2001 came to an end, we were comforted by the fact that we would be spending Christmas at home although I can hardly recall a moment of it, as we were otherwise distracted. By now the deployment schedule was in place. The two Auroras, carrying the boss and the other flight commanders, would depart between Christmas and the New Year, the main body, led by myself, would leave on 2 January 2002; however, the first of us to officially enter theatre was Captain Pleau, who left Christmas eve. His job was to find and book a hotel, engage the chandler,[12] start the ball rolling for all the equipment and infrastructure we would need, and grease the diplomatic skids. Denis, the lone man on the scene, took it all in stride.[13] He did so well, that he was the contact man for the chandler long after our arrival. For that he became known as the "King of Dubai", in homage to the Canadian sitcom.

The movement phase went exceptionally well with the exception of some last minute examination of the stores. Some critical items were missing, like the spare engine. Resupply had been discussed but not finalized. If the resupply periodicity was to be greater than three weeks (and at times it was), a spare engine would be critical if we were to maintain operations. This taught me two things: do not wait until the last minute to inventory the stores personally, and if possible, devolve as much as possible to the personnel not being deployed (those going had too much on their plate to worry about things others could handle).

I actually did try the latter by assigning the stores task to someone senior who was to remain in garrison. It met with little success. In fact, the various levels of commitment I found in those who were not deploying surprised me. Some of our folks did not seem to grasp the gravity of what was happening. Others could not give enough of themselves. Without reservation, I found the Wing administrative and logistic folks to be extremely dedicated as demonstrated by their repeated long nights and weekends to support an effort they ultimately would not participate in.

ARRIVAL IN THEATRE

The advance party greeted us at the airport offering the gift of cell phones. The extravagance of cell phones turned out to be both a blessing and a curse. As will become evident later, given our dispersal, good communications was a must. I came to despise them, however, and took to leaving it behind to the dismay of the boss who took to making "connectivity checks" on occasion.[14] Text messaging was particularly useful. Like e-mail back home, I could disseminate real time orders to multiple recipients in about 60 seconds. From there we transported to the hotel. I recall the city seeming so foreign, (and muggy). Later, we learned to get around like locals and took to calling new guys "pinkies".

The first few days in camp, up to and including the first mission flight were glorious. Upon arrival of the advance party just days before, the camp was nothing more than sand, some asphalt that formed an apron, and more sand. No water, no power, no fuel, and no infrastructure, such as a hangar in which to conduct the business of aircraft maintenance and mission planning. By the time I arrived there was at least a handful of trailers to provide some shelter. Over the next couple of days the airlift arrived via rented airlift, namely, an IL-76, an AN-124, and a 747, at a cost rumoured to be in the neighbourhood of $1 million apiece. The CC-150 Polaris could have handled some of the load but access to the hold demanded specialized loading equipment not found everywhere and its wheel configuration precludes landing at many airfields that require a minimum weight-to-wheel ratio.

I understand that strategic airlift is a hot issue in the Canadian Forces (CF) but if we are to become what we claim to be, a small but highly trained and mobile force, and given our current operational tempo, some form of strategic airlift seems to be required. I recall as we unloaded our equipment, the Detachment Chief Warrant Officer had us stand down mid-afternoon, as he was concerned about the heat. Although very well intentioned, he was perhaps later to recognize the futility of that gesture. At the time the temperature peaked at about 27 degrees centigrade, downright frigid in comparison to what was to come.[15]

If the first few days were glorious, the next several weeks were nearly so. The weather was still nice and the morale was high. We became a unit with a single purpose: the launching and execution of missions. Every action, every decision, was taken with that in mind; to this point we were alone on the camp. If I needed a piece of equipment the process was simple and relatively unchallenged - go down to the supply folks and let them know what was needed. Invariably it arrived in days. That would soon change.

The Tactical Airlift (TAL) detachment arrived in the camp in February. The competition for resources began immediately, starting with ramp parking spots, as we both wanted the Gucci spots for our air and ground crews. This seemingly small thing plagued my Roto. I had no quarrel with them; they had their job to do and so did we. Until March, despite the fact that two distinct and equal units occupied the camp, my boss was the camp commander, by virtue (I think) of his seniority in the deployment.

Even with the two units combined, we remained relatively small and certainly focussed. That too was rapidly to change.

March saw the arrival of the National Support Unit (NSU). All of the common logistic (log) / administrative (admin) functions (everything other than flying operations and intelligence) and, ostensibly, log/admin for the Navy fleet and the infantry battle group were subsumed by the NSU.[16] It is my opinion that over the course of the remainder of the Roto, the operational focus of the camp staff (not the two lodger detachments) was lost, utterly and completely. I cannot overstate this point. The NSU held daily meetings that lasted hours, during which, one insider told me, the subject of aircraft parts was never discussed in favour of the number of black floor mats to be issued per room.[17] The running joke became this: if the flying units permanently departed, the NSU would not notice their absence and the floor mat debate would continue. The terms "No Support Unit" and "Not on Sunday Unit" became widely used.[18]

It must be noted, for the most part, these are the same dedicated and hardworking folks I spoke of earlier. Only the organisation had changed. I cannot help but to wonder if the change in focus was directly attributable to the change in organization. Were the resultant loss of group cohesion and morale contributing factors? I can only assume this to be the case and that the new leadership failed to recognize the problem, or worse, failed to take action.

The locals accepted us with slight disdain but mostly indifference. Dubai is a city that is used to accepting western tourists and business people. Despite their inward feelings, shopkeepers (especially those at the "souks") greeted us with a forced friendliness you might expect from middle-eastern merchants. The Host Nation (HN) government, or so we assume, took some interest in our activities. Early on, there were several reported cases of picture taking from adjacent buildings and cars that seemed to circle the block for no apparent reason. Language was rarely an issue as most of those indigenous to the UAE and the expatriate workers spoke some level of English. Those who did not speak English spoke the language of money, which is often enough to get by. While there we were all to appreciate a different spin on the Israeli/Palestinian situation. The word "crusade" has a wholly new meaning in the Middle East. Most of us in Canada are perhaps not as worldly as we believe ourselves to be. Keep in mind that this is a relatively liberal gulf state; I can only imagine the culture shock of living somewhere even further from our western way of life.

The missions conducted by our aircrews fell into two general categories: Maritime Recognized Picture (MRP), which entailed populating a contact map for the coalition fleet, and Leadership Interdiction Operations (LIO), the identification and tracking of dhows fleeing across the Gulf of Oman.[19] Most of this is done at 200 feet over the water, day or night.[20]

SETTLING IN

There has been much talk over our accommodations for five of the six months. There is no question the hotel was extravagant, but hotels in Dubai follow the class system; they are made for the very rich, or the very poor. To my knowledge, there are no "Comfort Inns" or the like in Dubai. Also, the Taj (the name of the hotel) offered many of the things we were looking for in accommodation, it was large and therefore capable of housing all of us without concentrating us into one obvious, targettable zone. It had its own security, underground parking for the protection of the vehicles, and was inexpensive by comparison. We ended up in the hotel's "apartments", housing four to six personnel depending upon rank and gender. The only concession to rank was that senior officers, flight commanders, and flight warrant officers received their own room in the apartment, while the others doubled up. What Captain Pleau did not realize at the time that he selected the Taj is that he had picked what appeared to be the only "dry" hotel in Dubai.[21] As I remarked to Lieutenant-General Lloyd Campbell, then the Chief of Air Staff, during a visit, it may be a nice hotel, but it's a hotel nonetheless. The niceness of it all wears off pretty quickly.

I know I will never feel the sympathies of my Army brethren and rightly so, but living in a multi-star hotel had several large shortcomings. The hotel was 45 highway minutes from the camp that would eventually be named "Mirage". The logistics of shuttling 200 personnel, operating around the clock to support flying operations proved nightmarish. Aircrews worked a different shift than ground crews; the logistic folks also had their own separate shifts. Multiple buses, vans, and cars were needed to get us to and fro. Living downtown also presented opportunities for accidents and incidents. We had no Standard Operating Force Agreement (SOFA) with the UAE, only a verbal understanding that we would be treated with at least the same respect as white-collar expatriates if something should happen. Thankfully, nothing did, though we worried about what might happen if we found ourselves in the custody of the local law enforcement.

The local newspaper reminded us how readily criminals "confessed" once arrested. A picture of the so-called criminal(s) standing behind a table displaying his ill-gotten gains always accompanied the articles. Grim. Having said that I do not believe that we were in any great danger.[22] We travelled in pairs and were given regular intelligence briefs. Also, in my opinion, unsanctioned criminal activity of any magnitude was rare. The government seemed to have a pretty good grip on the population and its activities. I learned later that Roto 2 was held in lockdown for several weeks due to the political climate at the time.

Living so far from the camp also caused unwanted dispersion of personnel. If needed, the off-shift personnel would have to be rallied from all corners of the city and transportation would have to be found to get them to the camp. The mission leave period proved to be especially difficult on my guys. Earlier I stated that I wanted to bring only the minimum number of technicians to do the job. That presumed that we would all be living in the same geographic location. I assumed that if the on-shift crew needed assistance, it would be all too available from the off-shift guys who would be more than willing to pitch in for lack of anything better to do. Mission leave, when summed for three crews amounts to about two months, meaning that for two months I had only two crews in house. In that case, if you consider that the second remaining crew is dispersed 45 minutes away with little opportunity for transport, the on-shift crew was left to deal with the preparation, launch, and any and all snags. On more than one occasion I greeted the incoming crew at 0700 hours only to find them still there 24 hours later, looking somewhat haggard.

In that same mission-leave period we had significant difficulties in getting resupply through customs. Without available spares we resorted to whole-sale robbing of one aircraft to fit out the another. If the target aircraft became unserviceable, or if had flown too many hours, the parts were robbed back again. Robbing is an extremely cumbersome process that requires twice the amount of labour, paperwork, and functional checks. It also increases the risk of breaking the "serviceable" components in the process, thereby compounding the problem. By the end of the mission leave period the guys, particularly those who took the first leave window, were run ragged. I feel fortunate that all of the glassy eyed stares and shuffled walks did not result in an incident or accident. And so, I issue my second apology. Had I anticipated this problem, I would have taken more technicians.

By the end of the fifth month we moved onto camp, which immediately alleviated the problem. I discussed manpower with the maintenance flight commanders of subsequent rotations; they did not experience the problems that I did while employing the same number of personnel. To minimize the dispersal problems, the crews were encouraged to travel as a crew, with the crew chief, making themselves accessible by cell phone. They were also required to report their whereabouts to the Flight Warrant Officer.

Personally, dispersal itself was not my greatest challenge. At some point after deployment I (and I presume others do to) came to the stunning realization that I was wholly responsible for the welfare and safety of my technicians, far beyond the level of responsibility I was used to back home. Suddenly I became involved in all sorts of stress and relationship issues. Family matters (and there were several) that would have sorted themselves out at home eventually ended up on my docket. Even under the best of circumstances, family problems can be debilitating to the member; at such a distance they can easily cause the member great harm and, if left unchecked, ultimately affect the operation. In most cases my role was to be the one of social worker. I listened, I offered help wherever possible, and I ensured the member was closely supervised. Only in one instance did a personal problem lead to an authoritarian approach. One technician had left older children in the care of a friend. This arrangement worked well until a problem occurred where the technician requested to return home to address the issue. After assessing the situation, I felt that this would be a bad precedent to set and that this would lead to further requests to return home. I advised the technician that if taken, the trip would be one way and that I did not want the burden of a recurring problem of this nature. In this case, the technician opted not to return home.

Disciplinary problems overall were few and minor in nature. The Camp Commander routinely processed Summary Trials, mostly for alcohol consumption and violation of curfew. The members of my flight mercifully avoided those consequences by abstinence or cunning. No member of my flight was charged while deployed.

Eventually the resupply problem resolved itself but not before a stretch of three weeks I called Miracle Days. Parts had not been arriving. The HN was not allowing parts labelled "military" to pass customs and commercial air was failing, as there was a strike of some sort at Heathrow airport in England. Aircraft require lots of "TLC" - and parts. We were robbing to the point that there were several single point failures, meaning, if any one of several parts were to break, flying operations would abruptly cease. I distinctly recall getting up one morning and rehearsing my speech to the boss as I shaved. It started with, "I'm sorry Sir, we're grounded. I have no idea when we can resume flying", fully expecting it to come true. I did not have to give that speech that day, nor did I give it the next 19, at which point resupply finally arrived. Somehow the guys had pulled off the impossible. By any reasonable expectation, flying operations should have halted. For every one of those days I updated the status board behind my desk with the Miracle Day number.

Whatever your background, you may read the previous paragraph and wonder what the fuss was about. Miracle Days, what is the big deal? Collectively, we were there for only one reason - to put mission capable aircraft on station, on time. We took our part in that mission very seriously. For us, the end of Miracle Days *was* a big deal. To know that a few key parts threatened the mission and the gainful employment of the detachment was disconcerting. Even when regular airlift did resume, we found ourselves in competition with the Navy fleet and with the battle group for cargo space. Rumour had it that we, at times, did not receive aircraft parts because hockey gear and cigarettes had displaced them. That said, our supply problems did not rival those of our American counterparts.

Sometime in May I was given the opportunity to visit Bahrain, home of the USN 5th Fleet. There I was afforded the opportunity to see a different Arab State and get a sense of the size of the 5th Fleet headquarters. Bahrain is no Dubai. Quite clearly, its economy is not on par. Bahrain rates 55 in Gross Domestic Product (GDP) per capita behind all of the UAE (including the poorer emirates) at 32.[23] It had neither the glitz nor the infrastructure of Dubai. We stopped for a few minutes at the apartment building where many of the USN and liaison officers stay. Looking out the window of one of the apartments I was struck by how long and straight the road leading to the building was, optimally situated for a high-speed car bomb. One of the occupants of the building laughed it off by calling it "death valley" or something to that effect. Personally, I'd be looking for accommodations on the other side of the building.

The next morning we visited the 5th Fleet HQ. In the brief time I was there it appeared to me as organised chaos. The morning is largely taken up by briefings at all levels among many nations, all of them represented by their liaison staff. From there we visited CTG 57, the maintenance organisation that serviced the maritime patrol fleets belonging to the 5th Fleet. That was a bit of an eye-opener. The maintenance officer (Maint O), a pilot of the rank lieutenant-commander who spent most of his duty time at the HQ across town, accompanied us. Upon arrival, the Master Chief greeted the Maint O with a wave, to which the lieutenant-commander responded with a "how's it goin' Master Chief?" The Master Chief replied with "just fine Sir." It was easy to get the impression that this was likely the most they had to say to each other in the course of any given day. It was clear that the Master Chief ran the organisation but did not get the hands on management of the operation he would have liked. He explained that he spent most of his day on the phone tracking down parts, coming from various locations by various means. My parts problems, although big on my radar, seemed trivial next to his. I was then left to wonder how the Master Chief's occupation with chasing parts affected his operation.

I later related this to our USN exchange pilot, Lieutenant (USN) Van McIver. He explained that the relationship between the operators and maintainers of the USN is vastly different from our own. Their maintainers are much more independent and perhaps not as "customer focussed" as we are. Often, when a USN aircraft captain approaches the maintenance operations desk for an aircraft he is left to the mercy of what the Chief has, or wants, to offer. I could not see that working in CFB Greenwood or CFB Comox and was left feeling proud.

By end May, temperatures hit the 50 degrees centigrade mark. Before then I could not even conceive of temperatures in the 40s; 50 degrees is stinking hot, although I was surprised how well we acclimatized to it. Naturally, we took precautions - the guys handled the aircraft and tools with gloves. The surface of the tarmac exceeded 80 degrees centigrade. Hats were mandatory while on duty. In the mid-months, it was the high winds that caused the most grief. The sand storms could be merciless at times, forcing us to cease work until they relented. June and July for me were especially difficult. In addition to the heat, the humidity was stifling. Even worse at night, exposure to ambient air immediately resulted in a slick film that formed on the skin. Physical training for most, myself included, ceased sometime in the month of June. I learned that, while I could go for a run in the mid 30s, by 40 degrees I found it unbearable.

The aircraft also were not happy with the heat. The aircraft is normally cooled on the ground (during pre-flight checks and maintenance) by two means, the on-board Air Flow Multiplier (AFM), or by the portable air conditioning cart, more commonly known as a chilly cart. At around that time the AFMs were prone to catastrophic failure. Several conditions, including air starvation tended to over-speed the AFM impellor, causing the AFM to explode, taking some of the aircraft with it. Having this happen at home is bad enough; having this happen 3-6 weeks on the wrong end of the supply chain would be disastrous. The labour for repairs alone would cost several weeks. The whole repair would have grounded an aircraft for months. To avoid this situation I mandated the use of the chilly carts in lieu of the AFM.[24]

Unfortunately, the chilly carts were only rated to 40 degrees centigrade, a specification rarely met given their age. It simply was inadequate to the task. At best, they produced enough air to cool the avionics for short periods of time if they worked at all. This left no air for the crew during the pre-flight checks. This, and the inability of the Forward Looking Infrared Radar (FLIR) sensor to operate in the high heat drove our mission window to the early morning, ensuring a cooler, pre-dawn, launch. I ordered two new high-capacity chilly carts but they did not arrive until after our departure.

About the midpoint of the roto, my guys began to suffer from intelligence deprivation. One of the major concerns from the outset was the perception that our "value-added" in the war against terrorism would be minimal. This proved not to be the case, but the guys needed convincing. I passed my concerns to the boss, who, in turn, asked the liaison officer to come in from Bahrain and brief the detachment. The brief, given by Major Doug Baird, was invaluable to morale. Doug gave specific numbers of dhows intercepted at sea and suspected Al Qaeda members detained as a result of our patrols. The guys regained their sense of purpose and the value of our contribution was never again questioned. In hindsight, I think that some of their concerns stemmed from the lack of an apparent and traditional command structure.

From my perspective, the various chains of command were often complicated, made more so by the convenience of 24-hour satellite communications. Operational control was crystal clear; we took our mission orders from Canadian Task Force (CTF) 57, the maritime air arm of the USN 5th Fleet. Command was slightly less evident depending on the issue. We were under the command of Joint Task Force South West Asia located in US Central Command (CENTCOM), Tampa, Florida. They processed our larger log and admin issues, but when they became unresponsive on certain issues, like benefits, individuals resorted to dealing directly with National Defence Headquarters (NDHQ) through the informal "technical net", opening new, and sometimes permanent, lines of communication.

The issue of meal allowances was especially controversial and not fully resolved until more than a year after we redeployed. I could not hope to recall exactly what transpired but it went something like this: orders clearly specified our allowances for the first couple of weeks after which point they dropped sharply. Clearly not sufficient to live on, the boss appealed, citing established rates in other areas of the Middle East as precedence. When the response was slow to arrive, Lieutenant-Colonel Mitchell chose to maintain the rate at some middle point in the hopes that the issue would eventually resolve itself. The negotiations went back and forth for several months. Should the final decision turn against us, recovery action would certainly be taken. Even the threat of that happening was hard on morale. Nobody likes the idea of receiving allowances with one hand to have them taken away with the other. In the end, again that being one year after redeploy, the Director Compensation Benefits Administration (DCBA) figure was finalized at just *one dollar per day* less than the figure the boss had established. Naturally, recovery action followed. I estimate that less than $50,000 was recovered from Roto 0 personnel. I realize that every penny must be accounted for and that monies cannot be simply "written off", however $50,000 could not possibly account for the cost of issuing the recovery plus the impact to the loyalty of those members affected. It all seemed a bit trifling.

Mercifully, for technical and airworthiness issues, I was allowed to liaise directly with 14 Air Maintenance Squadron (my home unit) and the Aircraft Engineering Officer (AEO) in Ottawa. The AEO came to visit me before we departed in an effort to identify and resolve, in advance, any airworthiness concerns caused by operating remotely and independently.

Our conversation remained just on a verbal level - I failed to capture the outcomes in writing. Later I would realize that on those issues where I thought we had an understanding, we had none.

Over the course of the deployment we debated frequently but none more contentious than on the issue of aircraft washing, more technically called Corrosion Controls (CC). This seemingly benign activity caused me no end of grief and very nearly cost missions. At home the aircraft enjoy a CC every 30 days. It is an extremely valid and beneficial preventative maintenance program that staves off corrosion caused by salt water.[25] Unfortunately, we had no access to running water, making CC-level washes impossible, or so you would think. I was directed to "wash" the aircraft with a rubbing compound, something that I was not about to order my guys to do. I was spared the effects of insubordination by passing the problem to supply. I placed the demand for the compound as an Immediate Operational Requirement (IOR) and waited three months for it to arrive before I finally cancelled the order. The issue was eventually resolved as I took delivery of an off-the-shelf pressure washer. The aircraft were rotated every 60 days to allow a thorough wash before leaving and upon return. Any deviation from that schedule was dealt with by exception, meaning paperwork. On the 30-day mark I was to conduct a limited CC using the pressure washer.

This problem was further compounded by the environmental concerns over washing contaminants (grease, salt, dirt) into the sand. Despite the fact that I had permission from the HN to do so, I was hampered by Canadian environmental laws. I observed that firing depleted uranium into the desert seems not to be a problem, however, washing an aircraft, not unlike a larger version of your minivan, required an environmental assessment. I could not possibly count the number of e-mails this issue caused. My philosophy on this is: the aircraft were purchased for a reason. It is entirely possible they may form part of our inventory for 45 years and only see 10,000 hours of real-world operations as a fleet.[26] If using them for such a purpose causes longer-term problems that will need to be addressed then so be it. It's like the proverbial supply technician who tells you that he cannot give you the last pair of socks, because then he will not have any left on his shelf.

More often than not, it's the little things that manage to get under the skin. For me, force protection (FP) was another one of those things. During our deployment training force protection was discussed extensively – double rows of razor wire, guard towers, check points, vehicle searches and barriers, standing to, egress, etc.[27] Obviously this was further discussed with the Detachment Commander and, subsequently, higher HQ. Again, being amateurs in this end of the business we assumed that the Army in some form would support us by assuming all of the FP duties or at least by furnishing us with enough staff such that we could implement our own FP. Neither, it seemed, were forthcoming. Granted, there is not much point in making elaborate plans for FP without knowing where it is we would be setting up shop, however, the casual dismissal of a FP cadre was damaging to morale. Although, FP on this scale was never required, the inexperience of the security section in this area became evident. For example, the practice of sweeping the buses for bombs while entering the camp and not as they left the hotel, laden with passengers, I found particularly disconcerting. But as I said earlier, I don't believe that we were exposed to any great danger, at least on the ground. In the air was another story.

It is my sense that the aircrew suffered a greater risk. The CC-130 Hercules aircraft crews, who transited our patrol areas told of how they were regularly "painted" with radar from the countries that surround the Gulf. Our crews, lacking decent Electronic Support Measures in the aircraft, were oblivious to the potential danger. I was surprised by how well they accepted this risk. I suppose you have to place a great deal of faith in the aircraft to get you out of a situation and take comfort in knowing the crew you are flying with rival the best.

FINAL THOUGHTS

There is no doubt that my technicians enjoyed the work. It was the sort of work they signed up to do, aircraft repair and maintenance, without the distractions of secondary duties and the like. This dedication to the job and the lack of proper equipment brought out the "can-do" attitude. As an example, one of my crew chiefs took great pride in demonstrating how he changed a propeller using a forklift instead of a crane. Access to the tail was afforded by a set of portable VIP stairs mounted on the back of a pickup truck, or alternatively, a fork-lift fitted with a pallet wrapped in bubble wrap and a safety strap attached to the top of the hoisting assembly to hold the technician in place. We turned one sea container into a tool crib and another into a fabrication shop. There are other examples that perhaps should not be discussed. Without jeopardizing the safety of the aircrews or the airworthiness of the aircraft the guys effectively invented new ways of doing business.

The CP-140 community learned a tremendous amount from OP Apollo and is much better prepared as a result. I do not claim to know the full extent of the adopted Vanguard preparations but I know that a minimum number of aircrews and technicians are now required to be combat ready, screened, trained and generally "good to go" at any given time. TO&Es for various contingencies have been formulated and planning documents have been drafted. Perhaps most importantly, the community's collective mind-set has changed to accommodate the notion of long-term deployments, and to possibly austere locations.

As for the aircraft itself, although a great deal of time and money is being invested in the aircraft over the next 10 years, I fear for its survival. Consider this: the upgraded USN P-3 AIP aircraft made a significant contribution to Operation Enduring Freedom by providing operational commanders with a clearer picture of enemy positions within Afghanistan. USN P 3 Squadrons participated in attacks, firing Standoff Land Attack Missiles against Taliban and al Qaeda targets inside Afghanistan. The P-3s subsequently flew post-strike battle-damage-assessment missions and overland surveillance flights. Using real time imagery, this gave ground commanders a bird's eye view, day and night of the terrain where special operations forces were operating to dislodge Taliban and al Qaeda. Later, P-3s carried U.S. Navy SEALs (Sea, Air, Land) who assisted other Special Operations Forces (SOF) on the ground by using the aircraft's infrared sensors to pinpoint enemy al Qaeda troops hidden in caves. They then relayed information to other SOF teams on the ground and strike aircraft overhead.[28] This support was so effective and popular that it forced US Navy commanders to reconsider the aircraft's primary role, fearing that ground commanders would become too reliant on the aircraft for their own purposes.

The Air Force envisions that after the Aurora Incremental Modernisation Project (AIMP), the CP-140 will be at least as potent, and possible significantly more so, than the P-3 AIP. In short, in a few years we will have a significant capability that, I imagine, will be the envy of other nations. Having said that I worry that its capability may not be as valued within the Department of National Defence as it should be; that attention will instead be focussed on the "sexier" fighter aircraft. Bear in mind that it is Canada's only true C4ISR (command, control, communications, computers, intelligence, surveillance and reconnaissance) maritime patrol platform.

In conclusion, leadership in any situation makes all the difference. While in theatre I observed the leadership styles of various people and their effects. From the wing commander to my boss, other flight commanders, my flight warrant and the crew chiefs, I would like to think that I learned something. From the wing commander I saw how a battle staff meeting should be run - ruthlessly. It's the only way to run a meeting that includes a room full of leaders if you want to keep it on track. My boss showed me grace under pressure. With all that was at stake, he handled every aspect of the deployment and command of the camp with a quiet dignity and the occasional laugh. I would not have wanted his job, as it would have undoubtedly shortened my life span by several years. From my flight warrant, I observed a frightening combination of friendship and intimidation, both in perfect balance. He is exactly what you would want or expect in a chief warrant officer. My technicians taught me to abandon preconceived notions and that anything can be accomplished given the right motivation. Their performance was simply outstanding. The results speak for themselves. From everyone and everything there is something to be learned.

It's easy to remember those aspects of the deployment that gave us trouble and I hope I have not painted too bleak a picture. Certainly there were frustrating times but I would not trade the experience for anything. In the end we achieved an incredible 97 percent mission success rate, the highest in the coalition. This accomplishment garnered the Detachment considerable praise from the highest levels of both National and Coalition Headquarters. Most of the acclaim was heaped upon the technicians, who earned a Commander's Commendation for their efforts. Later rotos were equally successful if not more so, but I like to think that it was our labours that paved the way. Our success stymied our USN colleagues who actively sought our "secret," which was simply training, loyalty, and dedication.

ENDNOTES

1   A miscommunication regarding fuel delivery nearly caused us to miss the much anticipated launch time. The contracted fuel operator assumed we would need his services upon aircraft *recovery*, six hours too late. This caused the boss no end of concern.

2   The same engines used on the CC-130 aircraft, only right side up.

3   Although it pains me to admit this, while engaged in a mission, NAVCOMs are the hardest working guys in NATO. For eight hours at a stretch they huddle over their tacplots, collating info passed to them by the crew and issuing orders. I have every respect for someone who can do this job well.

4   The one notable exception was our participation in Operation Sharp Guard in the mid-1990s, however, that deployment was to a friendly P-3 base in Sigonella Italy and was treated little differently than an extended short-deployment.

5   It takes an enormous amount of tools, support equipment, and consumables to keep an old airplane flying. At one point the total kit to support the aircraft and personnel was estimated at more than 150 Herc chalks! I will leave you to do the math. DAG is the Departure Assistance Group - essentially, medical, dental, social, legal, and administrative in-clearance.

6   In the end, the torpedo load crews were not required as the role, and eventually the Host Nation, did not allow for armaments. Concern over this issue was so high we were not allowed to store sonobuoys in the external launch tubes.

7   Masirah Island, Oman was one of the location finalists. It is, quite literally, a 65km rock covered in sand.

8   The words "crew" and "team" are interchangeable in this context.

9   The expectation was that nothing would happen in their absence.

10   Just kidding about the Bedouins.

11   273 by my calculation. I recall him repaying *one* while returning to Canada through Athens. He may disagree with my arithmetic.

12   Chandler is an old naval term for someone who deals in ship supplies and provisions at the various ports the ship may visit.

13   Hotels, readily available, became the only option for housing, as the airlift required to transport sufficient tentage, etc, was cost prohibitive.

14   Once we were housed on the camp I ditched the phone. While in Dubai it was always glued to my hip.

15   Night time lows hit -8 degrees centigrade. At that point, not a problem on its own but the 30 degree temperature swings caused the guys to feel it all the more.

16   The fleet had its own support unit as early as November 2001, and nearly all of the log/admin functions of the battle group were integral to that unit.

17   It was hard to get any log/admin work done during these hours.

18   The day off policy for the NSU left an option of three days on which to take one's day off, Friday, Saturday, and Sunday. As the Host Nation "weekend" was Thursday and Friday, NSU pers invariably took Saturday or Sunday to avoid the crowds at the souks. For some reason, Sunday was favoured.

19   As it happens, our own Navy conducted many of the boardings.

20   The pilot's distinction of those two missions was summarized as "Fly to the Strait of Hormuz and turn left or right", respectively.

21   You may be surprised by the fact that not all hotels in the Middle East are dry - as were we. Most hotels in Dubai serve alcohol, it's just not evident from the outside.

22   A couple of personnel almost fell victim to scams, one of which would have certainly resulted in bodily harm.

23   From the CIA World Factbook Website. Canada ranks at 11.

24   Mandated by issuing an Operational Restriction on the usage of the aircraft.

25   Corrosion is bad.

26   No kidding, the unofficial estimated life expectancy of the aircraft is 2025, making it 45 years old upon retirement.

27   A hastily improvised course that combined the Individual Combat Skills course with theatre specific training included. Hats off to the cadre at 14 Wing that put this course together. Without knowing where we were going, they did their best to give us a meaningful course.

28   Gleaned from the VPNavy website, www.vpnavy.com

CHAPTER 8

COMPANY COMMAND IN THE THREE BLOCK WAR: NOVEMBER COMPANY – TASK FORCE KABUL, ROTO 0 - OPERATION ATHENA

Major Tom Mykytiuk

The intent of this chapter is to share my insights of company command in a challenging and complex theatre of operations. It is based solely on my personal experience and is not meant to be a dissertation on doctrine or a discussion on refining Army lessons learned. Rather, it is aimed at the captains and lieutenants who will someday command a sub-unit in operations as part of a larger Task Force. As such, if any of the insights I provide prove useful to future company, squadron or battery commanders, I will have achieved my aim.

The 3rd Battalion, The Royal Canadian Regiment Battle Group (3 RCR BG) deployed to Afghanistan as the "sharp end" of Task Force Kabul on Rotation 0 (Roto 0) of Operation (Op) Athena in the early fall of 2003. This signalled the start of Canada's commitment to the International Security Assistance Force (ISAF), created to protect the fledgling government of Hamid Karzai as he endeavoured to establish democracy and the rule of law in the wake of the Taliban. The Battle Group consisted of the Battalion Headquarters (BHQ), two light infantry companies, a Light Armoured Vehicle III (LAV III) company from 1 RCR, a combat support company, as well as a field engineer squadron.

The mission of 3 RCR BG was to assist the transitional government in building a secure and stable environment within the unit's Area of Operations (AO) in western Kabul. This mission was vague and indefinite, falling well outside the parameters of our doctrinal mission verbs. This ambiguity was a result of operating within the second block of what has been termed the termed the "Three Block War."[1] This concept argues that combat is only one element of conflict resolution, and in a war-fighting campaign designed to stabilize conflict areas, there exists the need to conduct humanitarian assistance, and stabilization operations concurrent with warfighting often at the same time in the same city – on three separate city blocks. This situation was aptly mirrored in Afghanistan.

At any given point in time, various aid agencies were involved in humanitarian relief; ISAF was focused on counter insurgency within the boundaries of Kabul; and forces assigned to Operation Enduring Freedom were engaged in combat operations against Al Qaeda along the Pakistan border. All three dimensions were linked and interrelated, and the effects of one were felt across the other two "blocks."

Given the nature and focus of our training, the idea of war fighting is easier for officers and Non-Commissioned Officers (NCOs) to grasp than the less defined concepts of humanitarian and peace support operations in an unstable environment. To assist the soldiers of my light infantry company – November ("N") Company (Coy), to adapt to this murky environment, I tried to identify clear "arcs of fire." Assigning tasks such as "conduct a minimum of two patrols within a Police District (PD) or, liaise with a sub-district police chief on a weekly basis" is much clearer direction that subjective terms such as "assist the transitional government in providing a secure and stable environment." As a company commander, your mission analysis should be the filter between the tangible and intangible. A complete understanding of the Commanding Officer's (CO) intent and end state is vital to determine where to draw this line. It is always important to remove as much ambiguity as possible.

Furthermore, adapting to the dynamic environment of the three-block war requires a degree of mental agility at all levels, supported by well developed Situational Awareness (SA). Cleary explaining the operating environment was critical to SA. This was enhanced by my inclusion as a sub-unit commander on the tactical reconnaissance (Recce) to Kabul. I was able to pass on first hand knowledge of the "Battlespace" and the tasks the soldiers could expect to undertake on my return to Canada. The involvement of sub-unit commanders in the tactical recce is imperative. Information is essential as it is fear of the unknown that generates stress and concern. A unit morale profile study supports these observations as the level of stress linked to the operating environment was significantly reduced once we had entered theatre and soldiers could gauge the threat first hand.

Another tool that enhanced SA prior to deployment was the Internet. Leaders within the company at all levels researched the news and current events in Kabul prior to our departure. Some went through the effort of posting news items pulled from the Internet on to the bulletin board in company stores. This trend indicated an interest in the AO that facilitated the passage of information. This was a marked contrast to an earlier mission to Bosnia in 1992 that I had been on where soldiers deployed with a deficit of information regarding the military/political environment they were entering. Use of the Internet should be encouraged as it enhances SA; however, it should not be used as a replacement for passage of information though the chain of command.

Once we had deployed to Kabul, the company's daily operations were largely at the section level, making it difficult to maintain cohesion within the platoons, as well as the company. This problem was compounded by the way the company was manned prior to deployment. The company that completed warfighting training during the Brigade Training Event (BTE) in Wainwright, Alberta was not the same company that deployed to Kabul. We received a number of augmentees from Oscar Company, the third rifle company in 3 RCR, as well as other units. These soldiers arrived after the collective training period of the BTE. As a result, new teams had to be built during the "theatre specific mission training" that was covered shortly before deployment. Again, this was at the section level and an indication of things to come. What would have been beneficial was another period of collective training as a sub-unit with formed platoons had time permitted. The 24/7 nature of collective training and its war fighting focus provides a company commander with frequent opportunities for interaction with soldiers and NCOs. It allows a company commander to be seen and exert visible leadership by the example he sets. I could walk around a defensive position and talk to the "gunfighters" in "N" Coy. It is difficult to achieve the same rapport with sections racing in and out of camp on varied schedules governed by a company patrol matrix. I was fortunate that much of the leadership remained in place from the BTE to provide a solid foundation for the company.

On another level, the mission environment fostered cohesion at the section level. Sections lived in a communal environment and worked together daily. As well, when time permitted, physical training (PT) was conducted at the section level to solidify team building. This emphasis on section patrol and activity provided an excellent opportunity to develop junior leaders. It also held the dangerous potential for micromanagement by supervisors. If mission command is to be effective, a balance is needed between effective supervision and micromanagement. To prevent this from happening, an effort was made to mentor the section leadership, by sitting in on patrol orders and monitoring rehearsal and Battle Procedure. This, coupled with a detailed reading of every company patrol report, gave me a good an indication of the strengths and weaknesses of the section commanders. I avoided the tendency to accompany section commanders on their patrols. This would have undermined their credibility with their sections, and would have impacted on their leadership, as decisions would have been deferred to me. Instead, I turned my company headquarters into another patrol section to augment the patrols tasks assigned in the company patrol matrix and lead these patrols as the patrol commander. This had a number of advantages. It alleviated the pressure on the platoons by filling gaps in the patrol matrix, and helped me gain an intimate knowledge of the complete company AO.

While the fragmentation of the company made it difficult to maintain cohesion, it was not impossible. There were some significant unit level operations that helped to solidify the company. As well, I held a company commander's hour each month. The questions that were asked were an excellent weathervane to gauge the state of morale within the company and identify the concerns that were foremost on the soldiers' minds. At the start of the tour the questions focussed on operational issues such as ranges, opportunities to test-fire and group weapons, concerns about security tasks and impact on patrols, and force protection issues. This was contrasted by the last one held prior to our redeployment when the questions were predominantly focussed on re-integration, redeployment timelines, leave and so forth. This change in mindset was an excellent reminder to the company leadership of the need for to remain focussed until the very end of the mission to counter any end tour complacency. The Officer Commanding's (OC) hour was also a platform for me to explain some of the issues that were developing in the theatre, such as the Loya Jirgha, reinforce why what we were doing was important, and the impact ISAF had on Afghanistan's future. Often as soldiers get bogged down in their daily routine they lose sight of some of the grander ambitions and aims of the mission. Identifying concrete examples of progress such as the increase in refugee traffic and construction in the city of Kabul helped the troops put their accomplishments into a larger perspective.

The nature of the company's tasks necessitated maintaining a 24-hour presence of some kind within our AO. We had to maintain the impression that ISAF could be everywhere and anywhere, at any given time. Patrols had to avoid routines and set timings. This regime was extremely demanding, especially when combined with routine camp security tasks, the impact of leave, and attrition from medical and compassionate repatriations. Rest and downtime had to be considered in planning as the company was expected to maintain this tempo for the duration of the tour. In the tasks I assigned the platoons, I tried to keep at least one section left out of battle for 24 hours. To make up the difference, shorter more frequent patrols were planned to maintain a visible presence, or patrols were sent out for a longer duration to cover more ground.

I took the approach that this was a 24 and 7 mission and treated my soldiers accordingly. When they were out on patrol or gate guard, they were on duty. Otherwise, their time was their own. This was difficult for some of the senior leadership to accept. They questioned why soldiers were in PT kit at 1000hrs. The answer was that they had been out on patrol until 0300hrs and were likely going out again at 2000hrs. An operation of this nature cannot have the garrison mentality that unfortunately crops up all too often on deployments like a desperate camp follower. Soldiers need their own time and their own space. This is difficult to achieve with communal living, away from home and family, and operating within a dangerous environment. There is no safe place to go, and you are never away from the watchful eyes of the chain of command.

It is counterproductive to try and fill their time with "training" or other activities when not employed on patrol, or other tasks. On all operations, there is a requirement for refresher training that cannot be ignored, however, these demands must be rationalized, and anything that does not support the mission discarded. We were fortunate to have an extensive PSP support network to see to the needs of the average soldier. Physical Fitness facilities were outstanding, and the living quarters and creature comforts " palatial." This was an important counterbalance to the stresses of deployment.

"N" Coy's operational tempo meant that patrols were led by section second-in-commands (2IC) and, occasionally, even 3ICs. Junior leaders had numerous opportunities to develop their skills and build up their confidence. This point was extremely important to counter the asymmetrical threat that was ever present on Op Athena. The risks faced by the company were manifested in hostile actions such as the mine strike on 02 October 2003 and the suicide bombing on 27 January 2004. This latter threat was the most difficult to deal with given its ostensibly arbitrary nature. The suicide bomber is the penultimate smart bomb. In the case of the 27 January bombing, none of the visible indicators identified by the intelligence community were evident. The enemy, it seemed, had the initiative. Soldiers want to act, to take the battle to the enemy instead of being on the receiving end. There was a need to overcome this disadvantage, to change reaction to action.

Again, passage of information was critical in these circumstances. I assembled the company and passed on all the details that I had regarding the incident on 27 January, as well as the subsequent suicide bombing of a British patrol a few days after the attack on our patrol. I did not notice any of the physiological effects of fear within the company. It is likely that each soldier felt some increase in anxiety and stress in leaving the camp confines on patrol; however, an advantage that we had was that this incident occurred late in the operational tour. The company had gained an intimate knowledge of its AO and had developed a rapport with the population who was generally sympathetic to ISAF. We had had opportunities to use the latest night vision equipment in the Canadian Forces (CF) inventory and train with the PAQ 2/4s issued in theatre. The soldiers were confident in their weapons, their equipment and their abilities. As well, active measures were taken to counter the threat of a suicide bomber such maximizing the use of side streets to avoid traffic congestion, increased use of LAV to transport patrols to debussing points, and most importantly, the collective leadership within the Battalion advocated a change in the weapons readiness states to weapons "readied," which meant a round in the chamber. This strengthened the sense that the troops had a "fighting chance." In these circumstances, leadership by example became even more important. After the restriction on the Iltis jeep was lifted, my company headquarters was one of the first "N" Coy patrols to hit the streets.

In addition to a dangerous operating environment, "N" Coy had to deal with the demands generated by "mission creep" and the inevitable changes that result as a mission matures. Fortunately, this disruption was fairly minimal during ROTO 0, with some notable exceptions. A direct result of the 2 October mine strike was a redrawing of the company AO and modifications to BG operating procedures. Most of the rural areas outside of Kabul became the responsibility of the LAV Company within the BG. Each of the two light infantry companies received three armoured vehicles with crews to patrol the rural areas that they retained on the city's periphery. These additional assets increased "N" Coy's flexibility and capabilities, but resulted in a new approach to our patrols. The vehicles provided protection, surveillance capabilities, and the ability to move complete sections. However, they inhibited the personal contact that the Iltis jeep facilitated. The result was more of a mixture of mounted and dismounted patrols in the outlying areas. Patrols would move by LAV or Bison AVGP (Armoured Vehicle General Purpose) to a debussing point and then patrol a village by foot. It also provided me with a more robust company reserve and the ability to establish self sustaining, protected night time observation posts in remote areas.

Midway through the deployment, the mission focus changed from providing a general stabilizing presence to directed operations aimed at taking offensive action against confirmed security threats within the ISAF AO. This included raids on suspect locations to capture terrorists or weapons, and surge patrols in selected areas to counter or deter a threat. In many respects this was a natural evolution of the mission as the BG developed contacts that could be exploited for information. It was a question of refining the "find" function of the "find, fix, strike" equation. Of the three, finding is most difficult as it takes time to gain the trust of the local population, as well as become comfortable and familiar with the operating environment. While the BG embraced this change, it resulted in new leadership challenges. There was now a requirement to become more involved with working with the indigenous police and security forces, as well as foreign military forces.

Operation Maverick was a company level patrol launched in response to reports of groups of armed "bandits" conducting home invasions in the largely Hazara populated Kabul suburb of Police District 14. This activity was centred around one of the sub-police districts, an area that could easily be covered by an infantry company. One of the underlying factors of all the BG directed operations was the requirement to involve the local authorities. ISAF was there to support them from the "second row," providing assistance and advice to the transitional authorities in the execution of their duties, instead of displacing them as the guarantor of security in Kabul. The Kabul City Police (KCP) had to be involved in the arrest of any suspects.

This posed a dilemma, as some of the KCP were not above suspicion of criminal activity. There was a need to maintain the "second row " approach while safeguarding operational security (OPSEC). The key to this balance was timing and centered on the question "when to bring the police in on the operation?" Too early and information could be leaked, jeopardizing the success of the entire mission, too late, and it would appear that ISAF was marginalizing the KCP.

ISAF always had maintained freedom of movement throughout Kabul and our patrols were a mix of patrols with and without the KCP. For Operation Maverick, I positioned a patrol within the vicinity of the Police District 14 HQ to provide liaison and transport of KCP officers if required. I intended to bring the police in only after we had contacted and detained any "bandits" and have the KCP conduct the arrests. A joint KCP/ISAF escort would then move them back to PD 14 HQ for processing. There was no change required to the Rules Of Engagement (ROE), as the force escalation procedures were adequate. My plan was to overwhelm any armed gangs with surprise and numbers. If we caught them breaking into a compound we would act at that point. If they had already entered a house we would contain the area to prevent any exit and then, with the KCP, go in and get the bandits. I grouped interpreters with the lead sections to provide an initial warning on contact, relying on night vision equipment and the cover of darkness to get close enough to the bandits to catch them unawares.

"N" Coy conducted two company patrols within the span of a week and discovered only deserted streets and dogs. Either the information we received was inaccurate or embellished, and the "bandits" never existed, or sufficient warning was given to these gangs prior to our movement to have them suspend their activities. On a number of other unrelated patrols, I observed pen flares being discharged as we passed a certain point along a main route but was unable to discover their source. It is likely that Camp Julien was under observation and these flares were used for early warning of a departing patrol.

In addition to the company patrols, I had the opportunity to plan three raids, execute two of them as part of a larger BG operation, and participate as an advisor on a third conducted by the French BG. I will not deal with the issues of intelligence gathering, legal aspects of targeting, or detention of suspects, but will instead focus on the tactical lessons learned during the conduct of these operations. OPSEC was especially vital to the success of these operations as was the integration of indigenous forces into the company. It was essential that the locals be seen as playing a key role in these operations and that it was not just an ISAF operation. The Afghan NDS (National Directorate of Security) could deal with cross jurisdiction issues that would consistently arise, as the local police were not notified prior to the raid. Likewise, these soldiers were valuable when dealing with civilians and police to minimize the impact a raid had on a local community or neighbourhood. In both of "N" Coy's raids there were non-combatants on the objectives that had to remain in the community in the wake of our action. To successfully integrate the NDS into the company and safeguard OPSEC, we had to quarantine the members of the NDS who participated in the raids with us prior to H-hour. These individuals were brought into the planning stage 24 hours in advance and were housed in Camp Julian. They were under an imposed communications blackout to prevent any information leaks once they were briefed on the plan. It was necessary to involve them early to go through rehearsals with the company. They were integrated into the sections and had to complete the same entry drills as the other section troops. They did not have the Urban Operations training that we had completed prior to deployment and there was the obvious language barrier.

Tactical drills are exactly that, drills, and there is no time for translation. We had to show them what they had to do and have them practice doing entry drills with us. As well, we had to get them used to wearing the protective equipment we gave them. These preparations were well worth the time as both raids the company conducted were executed without incident, resulting in a number of suspects captured, and a large weapons cache discovered and destroyed.

There are a few additional keys to the successful completion of "N" Coy's operational tour in Kabul that merit discussion. One was the issuing of orders to the company as a whole rather than just the company orders group. I used this whenever possible for the company missions we conducted on Roto 0. This approach ensures that all soldiers are aware of the end state and the commander's intent, and can do their part to achieve these aims. As well, it aids in speeding up battle procedure, a crucial point as there never seems to be enough time, by broadcasting important features regarding the threat, the many points needing coordination, and the details of logistical support to the entire company. This does not marginalize the platoon commanders as it frees them up to focus on their tasks and enables the issuance of abbreviated orders to their platoons, speeding up the process up at their level. All my platoon commanders were advocates of this approach. As well, as a commander you can gauge the body language of the troops within the company and any questions they raise can be answered in this forum for all to benefit. Along these same lines, models are worth the time required to make them properly as they give more clarity to an objective than one-dimensional photographs or drawings. I used models to great effect as part of the planning for Direct Action operations.

Snipers were essential to both Op Maverick and to Direct Action missions. In both cases, they were positioned to provide observation and force protection. As expert recce patrolmen, they can provide more than just surgical shooting. Due to their highly developed field skills, it was possible to insert them in the early phases of these missions to provide continuous area or point surveillance, and develop identified objectives in real time. This presented them with the task of establishing observation posts within an urban environment, and overcoming the challenge of barking dogs, or curious locals, amongst others. Adapting to the complex terrain of an urban environment will likely become even more relevant as the trend towards missions in densely populated trouble spots increases.

Another factor that cannot be overlooked is the use of language assistants or interpreters. They are vital assets to any patrol or raid. If you cannot communicate with the local population, passage of information is non-existent. However, they are usually young adults or teenagers without any military experience. Working with western soldiers creates a degree of culture shock, so some knowledge of their culture is important to minimize the effects of this. As well, as one mentioned to me, "they have to live here after we leave." It is important that they safeguard their identity on raids and some degree of force protection has to be provided them. They will normally be forward with the commanders so their safety must be considered. It is not the same as having a fellow soldier next to you. However, once you are confident in their abilities they are key pieces to the information puzzle. They can advise you on nuances of the speakers, background conversations, or simply what is being said on the local news. They give you a good feel for how the population reacts to certain actions, or their sentiments about you and you soldiers. It is key to remember to include them when estimating tasks.

A resource that remained largely underutilized within my company was the civil military cell (CIMIC). This group can be vital to information gathering and force protection. The challenge that is posed to a company commander is how to lever CIMIC projects to gain information or enhance force protection. I relied on the CIMIC staff and the platoons to identify worthwhile projects to spend money on, or locations where some self-help initiative could be completed with assistance from ISAF. The projects, however, were not focussed towards some overall plan to achieve information that could be used for directed operations, or force protection. This shortfall was compounded by the fact that a comprehensive CIMIC plan did not exist at the battalion level. There was no well-defined end state in this respect. I am not advocating using aid as a weapon – winning the hearts and minds of the host population is an important objective. However, the way CIMIC projects were delivered and where they were focussed could have been done more intelligently and effectively than they were in my company AO. This is largely because CIMIC is outside the scope of the type of combat operations I was trained in. Nonetheless, it has gained far more relevance within the context of the three-block war, and company commanders should exploit it for the valuable tool that it is. I cannot offer too much to resolve this, other than recommend commanders fully understand what CIMIC can offer and be imaginative in its application.

My experience in Kabul was challenging and rewarding. I was fortunate to command a light infantry company on an exciting new mission. I was blessed with an excellent Company Sergeant Major (CSM) and motivated professional NCOs and soldiers. As a company commander I enjoyed an unparralled degree of freedom of action given to me by a CO who believed in mission command and trusted his sub-unit commanders to get on with achieving his end state. It was the best job in the Army.

As in many cases, the most valuable lessons learned, are learned through experience. My experience in Kabul can be summarized in a few salient points. While these may appear to be self-evident truths they are worth reviewing as they were in many respects key to the success of "N" Coy's mission:

- Stabilization operations are not as clearly defined as war fighting. To aid soldiers in adapting to these missions, strive to minimize the grey areas with clear and simple direction. Your mission analysis should be the filter between the tangibles and the intangible.

- Operating within the context of the "Three Block War" requires a degree of mental flexibility at all levels. SA is key to this flexibility. The Internet is a valuable source of information and can be used effectively to enhance SA. Its use should be encouraged at all levels; however, it does not replace passage of information through the chain of command.

- With missions that are often a section commander's battle, it is difficult to achieve and maintain sub-unit cohesion. Much of this cohesion must be built prior to deployment through collective training opportunities at the platoon and company level. There is a need for visible leadership at the company level and occasions such as company commander's hours should be maximized. As well, look for opportunities to work at the company level whenever possible. Take an active role in mentoring and developing your subordinates through monitoring of Battle Procedure and patrol debriefs, however, let the section commanders command their sections when they leave the confines of the camp. Consider employing your company head-quarters as a patrol to gain the SA of your AO instead of imposing yourself on section patrols.

- Look for ways to mitigate operational tempo. Treat 24/7 operations as exactly that. There is no room for a garrison mentality at the company level on operations.

- Soldiers need to feel able to act to deal with a threat. Look for active instead of passive measures to counter the threat. Strive to give them that "fighting chance."

- When operating with indigenous forces, OPSEC must still be considered. A balance must be found between how much information can be shared and when to ensure the success of a joint operation. As well, rehearsals are key to these types of operations to address the shortfalls in the training of the indigenous forces as well as the obvious language barrier.

- Delivering orders to the entire company maximizes the sparse time that is normally available for Battle Procedure and ensures that your intent and end state are outlined to every soldier in the company. It does not marginalize your platoon commanders and instead leaves more time for Battle Procedure at the platoon level. Use models.

- Snipers are valuable assets when employed in support of company operations. It is imperative to understand their capabilities and limitations. They are expert recce patrolmen and can provide more than surgical shooting. However, they must be prepared for the challenges of operating in complex terrain such as urban centres.

- Language Assistants are vital to operations. Ensure they are part of your troops to task estimate.

- Be aware of everything that CIMIC can do for you. Be imaginative in developing an end state for what you want to achieve with your CIMIC resources that can lever your tactical objectives. It is too valuable an asset to marginalize.

As a parting shot, I would like to see that overused, media invented word "peacekeeper" removed from our contemporary lexicon. It is a product of the Cold War and brings with it associated expectations and clichéd images. The world and the Canadian Army has moved past the era of separating warring sides by parking between belligerents with small arms and trucks painted white. We face a world of failed and failing states, and asymmetrical threats without defined boundaries or borders. We must be prepared to operate across a full spectrum of conflict. If we must categorize our missions, call them counter insurgency operations, or low intensity conflict, or more accurately, security and stabilization operations. But do not call them "peacekeeping."

Peacekeeping suggests a passive non-invasive presence operating in a benign environment. Peacekeeping advocates that nobody will get hurt, and that everybody involved welcomes us without malice. The reality is somewhat different. We have seen that in the execution of our missions, Canadian soldiers will be hurt and some will lose their lives. We have witnessed that our soldiers will be operating with the local authorities to deter and react to threats to security and stability. Photographs of detainees with zapp strapped hands and hoods on their heads may appear in newspapers, and discussion about the Geneva Convention not applying to these missions will ensue. But that, quite simply, is the world of failed and failing states - the world of the asymmetrical threat, and the world that the CF and, by proxy, the citizens of Canada must contend with. This is the world that the captains and lieutenants of today will face as the company, squadron, or battery commanders of tomorrow.

ENDNOTES

1   Former USMC Commandant Charles Krulak coined the phrase – "three block war" where soldiers will be expected to provide humanitarian assistance in part of the city, conduct peacekeeping operations in another, and fight a lethal mid-intensity battle in the third part – all on the same day, all in the same city. See Charles C. Drulak, "The Three Block War: Fighting in Urban Areas," *National Press Club*, Vital speeches of the Day, 15 December 1997.

CHAPTER 9

THE KEYS TO MISSION SUCCESS:
"C" COY IN AFGHANISTAN

Major Kevin Caldwell

In the summer of 2003, "Charles" Company ("C" Coy), a Light Armoured Vehicle (LAV) III Company from the 1st Battalion, The Royal Canadian Regiment (1 RCR) was attached to 3 RCR (a light Infantry Battalion) for one month of Theatre Mission Specific Training (TMST). This was followed a month later by a deployment to Afghanistan as part of Operation ATHENA Roto 0. At the time, the Coy totaled 135 all ranks, with 16 LAV III, six Iltis jeeps and, depending on serviceability, one light support vehicle wheeled (LSVW) for the Coy Quartermaster's (CQ) use.

There were three officers, including myself, in the Coy headquarters (HQ) element, as well as the CQ and transport staff totaling seven other ranks. The three platoons in the Coy were comprised of one officer each and 37 other ranks. We were allocated the normal quantities of support weapons and the like, and each platoon could deploy one 84mm Carl Gustav anti-tank (AT) weapon, ERYX AT missiles and a 60mm mortar. Being mobile and having armour protection, as well as the ability to sustain ourselves for a short period of time, I knew that our new Commanding Officer (CO), Lieutenant-Colonel Don Denne, could call upon the Coy at a moment's notice to execute tasks once deployed. At the start of our rotation, our mission was "to assist Afghan authorities in maintaining a secure environment within boundaries, from 21 August 2003 to contribute to the International Security Assistance Force (ISAF) desired end state of a secure and stable Kabul." Later, this mission changed to also incorporate the conduct of directed operations in support of the Kabul City Police and the National Directorate of Security. The challenges stemming from that transition will be discussed later.

In all, we faced many challenges during TMST and throughout our six months overseas. The first challenge was incorporating 40 new augmentees that were attached to "C" Coy just days prior to the TMST. Overseas, we overcame many hurdles in slowing skill fade, and in minimizing the fear that was felt especially after the suicide bomber attack. Other concerns revolved around the soldiers' morale, the ambiguity of the mission from time to time, intelligence gathering, and building confidence from section to battalion level operations.

Leadership and organizational behaviour literature commonly points out that effective leadership exerts an influence on followers in a way that achieves organizational goals by increasing and enhancing satisfaction, initiative, innovation, efficiency and effectiveness, as well as commitment of followers or subordinates. At the start of the mission, my intent and overarching aim was to build our sub-unit confidence and to constantly challenge all leaders and soldiers to improve their leadership abilities, and critical thinking skills. I knew this goal would require much more work and self-directed initiative on everyone's part, and it was true.

As the Officer Commanding (OC) the Coy, my job was to train the Coy second in command (2IC), LAV Captain, and platoon commanders so they could step in and make decisions in my absence. In regard to the mission, I determined that we needed detailed information concerning the terrain, the local people, the Afghan Militia Forces (AMF), the Afghan National Army (ANA), their police structure, as well as the need to develop human intelligence (HUMINT) contacts. We found out early on that without intelligence all we would accomplish was the conduct of low level presence patrols and being physically seen in the area of operations (AO). Yes, we reassured the locals with our presence but, aside from that, we would not affect more permanent change.

In addition, besides developing my leaders and commanding the Coy, intelligence gathering was one of my primary aims. I believed it would present the Bn with the means to identify targets for directed operations, which were conducted successfully later in the tour. As well, I believed that we were obliged to give the Royal 22nd Regiment (22eRR), who were scheduled to replace us, a much more detailed handover than what we had received when we arrived. The only way for that to occur was by mastering our AO.

For our ultimate success, I knew I could not rely solely on an authoritarian style of leadership. Rather, I chose to set standards and enforce them rigidly, but also to frequently ask for my subordinates' advice and input. I refused to accept a minimalist approach to my duties and expected others to perform in kind. Many of our challenges in Afghanistan were overcome by effective leadership, from top to bottom, and demanded excellence, accountability, professionalism, enforcement of discipline, leading from the front, superb team building, and lastly constant communication.

At the start of TMST, I was faced with commanding a Coy that was comprised of more than 40 new personnel, two new platoon commanders, a new Coy 2IC and not enough time to conduct company level operations. TMST focused on section level tasks, Rules of Engagement (ROE), cultural awareness and the like, but not platoon and company level operations or war fighting. Yes, during the Brigade Test Exercise (BTE) in CFB Wainwright we did have the time to conduct those activities, but our order of battle (ORBAT) had changed. Herein lay the challenge. Therefore, during TMST the company sergeant-major (CSM) and myself stressed to the leaders the importance of making sure that everyone was suitable to deploy overseas. In some cases, after observing and supervising individuals in the execution of their duties, I recommended leaving them behind so they could further increase their skill sets in Canada instead of in an operational theatre. In addition, given the limited time, the Coy focus quickly shifted to ensuring all soldiers were administered correctly for deployment. As such, the major challenge of bringing the new company together, as well as fully integrating it into a light infantry battalion, had to wait until we were deployed in Afghanistan.

Once deployed overseas, we conducted handovers with our German counterparts and, for the most part, all went smoothly. I can remember one instance when Warrant Officer George (9 Platoon (Pl) 2IC) was being shown the Paghman area (West of Kabul) by his counterpart and a bridge was washed out. At that time, he was in a German vehicle and the other commander told his driver in German to drive through the riverbed to reach the other side. Once that occurred, Warrant Officer George told the commander in no uncertain terms, with as much tact as he could gather, that they would stick to the cleared route trace. The point to note is that while we may conduct operations in a certain way, not all armies do the same. Nevertheless, all handovers for the Paghman Area and Police District (PD) 5, located just East of the Paghman area, went as planned. Since the Coy was given two areas to patrol, I had decided earlier to allocate PD 5 to 8 Pl, commanded by Lieutenant Greg White, and Paghman to 9 Pl, commanded by Lieutenant Carl Bennett. I kept 7 Pl, commanded by Lieutenant (later Captain) Kris Reeves[1], as my floater / reserve. As Kris had the most experience, I felt he could easily adjust to the two different areas whenever called upon, and he never failed to rise to the occasion.

Immediately after deployment, I issued our Standard Operating Procedures (SOPs) so that the new additions to the company would know how operations were to be conducted; how vehicles were to be packed for patrols; the amount of ammunition to be carried by individuals, and so on. Before doing so, I asked my Orders Group (O Gp) for input on how best to achieve this aim - then issued direction. I understood that each of the platoons would have their own ways of conducting business and accepted that fact, as they needed some autonomy to organize their own affairs. As WO George stated, "SOPs were sorted out at the platoon level but at times it had to be put in place by the OC via the chain of command."

When I had to impose SOPs, communication was paramount so that everyone understood my intent. When this occurred, two-way communication was the key to getting everyone onboard. However, this could not have occurred without the diligence of CSM Simmons as he ensured all direction was adhered to.

For patrolling, the CO wanted all companies to conduct a minimum of three patrols a day providing 24/7 coverage in AO. Coupled with that requirement, I directed that each platoon would conduct one platoon operation weekly to solidify their cohesion and confidence. At the time, I was concerned that if all we conducted were section presence patrols my leaders would lose the ability to conduct platoon and or company level operations. Further, I believed that the platoon commanders would lose touch and credibility with their sections. While this was not well received by some of the platoon commanders, I did communicate why they needed to command their sections a minimum of once a week in order to practice battle procedure, to take ownership of their districts, and other critical skills. When speaking with Lieutenant White after the tour, he told me that, while he hadn't always seen the need for weekly platoon operations, in hindsight, he now believes that it proved to be the absolute best way to master battle procedure and platoon commanding. Forcing the platoons to conduct both platoon and company level operations helped to reunify the company after it had absorbed over 40 augmentees prior to TMST training.

The other initiative I used to build the Coy's cohesion early on was to progressively assign challenging responsibilities to my leaders through the issuance of weekly tasks that they were allowed to complete under supervision. This was done at all levels within the Coy so that I could gauge their effectiveness but also to prepare the Coy for the impending rotational leave plan.

Coupled with weekly tasks, my O Gp was routinely involved in the planning process before the Coy conducted surge operations. Captain Steve Champ remarked, "involving the Coy 2IC and LAV Captain in all planning processes early on ensured that redundancy was built in for the leave period. Without this involvement, I would not have been as capable of executing operations in the AO while the OC was away." I had involved my 2IC in prior planning cycles, in drafting orders and in commanding the company so that he would have the platoon's confidence and trust in my absence. As it turns out, Captain Champ performed with excellence in executing three-company level operations, as well as in developing contingency plans for two more operations. I can remember speaking with the operations officer and the adjutant when I returned and asking them how my 2IC performed. They both said Captain Champ performed exceptionally well, particularly given his lack of formal command and staff training at the Army's staff college in Kingston, Ontario. They noted he displayed detailed planning skills, a firm logical thought process, and the ability to effectively argue and support his plan.

There were many other leadership challenges. In attempting to slow the inevitable skill fade caused by constant presence patrolling, I gave my commanders the leeway to plan their own refresher training during their Quick Reaction Force (QRF) cycle. When tasked by the Bn HQ with camp security, the QRF task and / or the standing operations tasks for a three-week period, I designated that each platoon would stay on each task for one week. When directed, the platoons came up with detailed plans for their refresher training during the QRF task and after some revisions the plans were finalized. Later, the Battalion used portions of Captain Reeves' QRF refresher training plan when they issued direction detailing the type of training to be conducted. Skill fade did occur in Afghanistan, but its worrisome effects were mitigated with training during the QRF cycle. As well, during a normal patrol schedule, the platoons conducted 30-60 minutes of refresher training daily. However, one area in which skill fade did occur was in the lack of live fire training. Soldiers can only conduct dry training so many times. Real confidence building only occurs when firing live rounds. I know the Battalion tried to resolve this issue many times – the lack of training was not for want of trying.

During the tour, I pushed the platoon commanders to take responsibility for training their own soldiers. Yes, I could have directed them to do everything step by step, but I wanted them to take responsibility for training their own soldiers and to learn from their mistakes. Captain Williams remarked, "the OC challenged the platoon commanders at their level by demanding more than the conduct of routine framework patrolling." Throughout the tour, I forced the platoon commanders to think constantly, and to plan effectively. My underlying goal was to develop their skill sets as leaders so that they could accomplish any mission with minimal to no guidance. "[The OC] generally let us come up with our own plans and execute as we saw fit, unless someone's plan was *right out of 'er*, then he would stop it," Lieutenant White stated. However, this did not only apply to the platoon commanders. Right down to the lowest levels, soldiers were given tasks that in Canada a sergeant would be expected to perform. With reduced manning due to the rotational leave plan and other battalion and / or brigade taskings, we needed to be able to rely on everyone. And, all soldiers rose to the challenge by commanding vehicle check points (VCPs), traffic control points (TCPs), coordinating with the locals, and any other activity assigned to them. I can remember many times being proud of the soldiers when I saw them conducting their duties with tact, professionalism, patience, and with a sense of purpose. The bottom line is that leaders must give their subordinates the freedom to make decisions, to take ownership, and to make mistakes all without penalty. If not, they will never strive to use their initiative or to make a decision. Allowing my leaders and soldiers to use their initiative helped forge the Coy into a much stronger sub-unit for the CO to use as he saw fit.

Developing the soldiers' confidence in their leadership was another one of the keys to our success. Soldiers will not always agree with the plan, but if they know the plan down to the last detail they will be able to respond with confidence to the *fog of war*. In planning most operations, all leaders were involved in the decision making process. I wanted the commanders to take some ownership of the company level plans so that they would not just be following orders. I felt if they had some input then they would more willingly perform their duties and sell the plan to their subordinates.

However, there were times I could not follow this approach due to time constraints. The point to note here, is when you can ask for input, and involve your subordinates, they normally have good ideas.

Coupled with joint planning, I stressed planning to the infinite detail for all phases of our operations. For success, the company welcomed specialist elements like engineers and medics, as they were an asset. Once orders were issued, the majority of time was spent rehearsing all contingencies. Captain Reeves noted, "the [OC's] emphasis on rehearsal instilled confidence in the Coy and helped to ease the pain when we were 'stop dropped." Rehearsals helped to promote professionalism and we knew we could receive a mission, plan and rehearse it then put it on the shelf until given the order to execute." Lieutenant White said that, "[the Coy] rehearsed operations to the point where you asked the privates the scheme of manoeuvre and they knew it." Constant rehearsals and detailed planning gave my soldiers and leaders added confidence that we could execute any mission when called upon. It helped strengthen the company and build our group cohesion.

I demanded the platoons take ownership of their districts and plan their own operations given the intelligence we might have gleaned. This was my mission focus for the whole tour. In order to be successful at all levels, we needed to approach our overarching mission with more than a patrolling mindset. I pushed the platoons to develop HUMINT sources. After all, if we did not, how could we really determine what the people were thinking? In Afghanistan we were vulnerable to attack 24/7 and we could only stop Taliban type supporters if the locals told us who these people were, and where they lived.

As a result, the platoons gathered a tremendous amount of information that was collated by the Coy Intelligence non-commissioned officer (NCO), Master-Corporal Arsenault. He did a fabulous job in making linkages when reviewing the patrol reports and through his actions he ensured the intelligence officer and his staff were aware of those linkages.

Again, I believed we had to do more than patrol our AO. And, only with hard intelligence could we conduct direct action operations in the future. This emphasis also gave the platoons another focus, which enabled them to use their own ingenuity, to accomplish my aim. As Captain Aaron Williams stated, "the process of developing personality profiles and tracking local issues and sentiment gave purpose to their patrols." Captain Reeves observed after the tour, "Our emphasis on information gathering gave focus to our operations."

This was proven on many occasions and especially on one when I was called over to the All Source Intelligence Centre. While being briefed on a potential operation, I leaned over to the intelligence officer, Captain Cody Sherman, and told him that we have pictures and personality profiles produced for the targets in question on which he was briefing everyone. This would not have been possible without the active interest of the platoons in performing their duties.

Another major leadership challenge was the scale of operations. This is not new or unique. Whenever on tour, the operational *tempo*, and especially the managing of it, will always be a challenge. There is never enough time to do everything a commander wants to do, so commanders must pick and choose their focus points and then stick to them. The balance for maintaining tempo is that it must be both sustainable and aggressive at the same time. Each platoon performed three patrols a day and they had one day off a week. However, on that day off they also performed their weekly vehicle maintenance so... in reality it was only a half-day off. The tempo was also managed by the daily routine. Each day the same thing occurred and as Captain Reeves stated, "routine was the key. Missions and operations could come and go but certain steps were rarely overlooked and that helped. Morning briefings, and weekly maintenance, all helped to maintain structure for the soldiers."

In order to balance the platoons' tempo during the maintenance days, the Coy HQ and Pl HQ LAVs would conduct patrols and liaison visits to fill in for shortfall every Friday. As well, the company 2IC and LAV Captain were directed to get out of Camp Julien for a *break*, to participate in AO familiarization, as well as to observe platoon operations. Furthermore, they would attend the CO's morning O Gps once a month so that they could become familiar with how he operated as well as develop confidence when responding to his questions. I also did this so that he could get to know them better and have confidence in their abilities.

The CSM, Master Warrant Officer Simmons was also instrumental in advising me of any problems with the tempo of operations and his guidance was one of the keys to maintaining a positive working atmosphere. I also spoke with the soldiers frequently and conducted OC hours where the soldiers were encouraged to speak freely so that I could allay their concerns where possible but also to reinforce my intent regarding operations. OCs and Pl commander's hours were very important during the tour and as Warrant Officer George reminded me, they should never be cancelled.

In Afghanistan, we could have been attacked anytime. By that I mean we used the same few routes daily to exit and enter the camp, we patrolled every day, and we dismounted from our LAV's to patrol the same areas. However, one way I determined to mitigate that threat was to give away as much civil military cooperation (CIMIC) assistance as we could without unduly affecting patrolling. Some in the company were concerned that it was taking away from our primary focus of patrolling, but I believed that the giving of aid would lead to security, which could lead to information. That is, information and intelligence may give us more security in the future and or may provide us with details in order to conduct direct action operations. Again, the greatest asset we had to try and develop was the trust of the local people. They knew who the extremists were but in many cases they were afraid to tell us, and giving aid was one way I believed we could get them to be beholden to us.

Now let us not be confused. Aid distribution was not contingent on getting information first - then giving aid - but rather the other way around. I felt that Afghanistan was a multidimensional operation and for our success and security we needed to use all factors at our disposal. Yes, our mission was to provide a safe and secure environment by patrolling, but patrolling alone would not accomplish that goal. While some did not agree with my methods, they still got on with it because I communicated my intent whenever I could.

After the Battalion suffered its first fatalities, I remember the CO and the operations staff speaking about how to increase our presence in the Jowz Valley[2] where the improvised explosive device (IED) incident occurred. To affect an increased presence, we patrolled more in that area and looked closer at our CIMIC activities. I can remember escorting a heavy lift vehicle wheeled (HLVW) 10-ton truck full of aid and giving it to the local Malik for distribution to his village. At that time, while surrounded by many villagers, the Malik told me that my soldiers would always be safe in that area. I cannot say for sure that it helped to protect my soldiers or others in the Battalion, but it did enable me to establish a closer relationship with the Malik, which lead to some concrete intelligence later on. "To be honest," Lieutenant Carl Bennett admitted later, "I was not a big fan of the CIMIC operations but the results they provided the company were invaluable. The locals became more tolerant of our presence and in some cases downright happy to welcome us into their homes whenever patrolling."

By giving the Malik aid, we were able to establish a closer relationship in an area that was not supportive of ISAF. We were able to demonstrate that ISAF did not only patrol but they actively cared about the people. We gave them hope, which they were lacking. Captain Champ observed, "CIMIC operations were tied directly into our intelligence gathering operations, in making personal contacts, and our success depended on it." He added, "CIMIC was just another venue for the Coy to accomplish our mission. I tied all our efforts together; it gave us a sense of purpose we required to maintain momentum. It ensured everything we did, from [CIMIC] to police training, contributed to the aim."

Stress and fear were ever present in Afghanistan. Everyone in the Coy hoisted aboard this reality after one operation when we were given the dispositions and actual strengths of a number of Afghan Militia Forces. Yes, we had the technology, new weapons systems, and the LAVs and all their attributes (e.g. firepower, mobility, protection, communication, thermal night sights), but to a large degree, the AMF and ANA had heavy armour like tanks, which we did not. Stress was particularly felt after the two instances where our comrades died in the line of duty. Although we had more protection than the light infantry soldiers, we too had to dismount to conduct patrols and conduct liaison visits. Thus, the soldiers naturally still felt vulnerable. However, to combat the stress as Captain Reeves recalled, "we kept focused on the mission, we used the section commanders and 2ICs to maintain eyes on the junior soldiers. Nothing fancy here, just good leadership at all levels."

The key here was for leaders to lead from the front especially after the suicide bomber attack. After the attack, the CO directed that only mission essential patrols leave the camp. After a period of time I directed Master-Corporal Tedford, my crew commander and main signaller, that we would be leaving the camp for a patrol. I remember speaking to the CSM, and we talked about the need for us to lead by example and go on a patrol. I can remember thinking that I may be placing my crew in harm's way but I believed there was an overarching need to be seen outside the gate to give the soldiers confidence in our mission, in their leaders, and our *raison d'être*. Another instance where this occurred was when I was away on leave. While away, a Rocket Propelled Grenade (RPG) was fired near one of our section vehicles on patrol near an AMF observation post (OP). At the earliest opportunity Captain Champ, as the acting OC, commanded a vehicle and went to the Afghan OP and calmly assured them that the next time one of our patrols was fired on, the OP would be receiving a sabot round of ammunition from our 30mm cannon in kind. As it turned out, we never were fired upon again.

Fear was a constant, and leaders at all levels led by example to mitigate its infectious spread. In an operational theatre, leaders need to be seen out on patrol, conducting routine vehicle maintenance on their vehicles, conducting refresher training and as Warrant Officer George so elegantly phrased it, "not [be seen] sitting behind their desk." He also said, "taking the lead in establishing time for the soldiers to do maintenance and doing it with them and not just delegating and disappearing, helped to build a strong team." I can remember the time the CSM and I were up armouring our vehicle with our crew and I overheard the maintainers say they were surprised the OC and CSM were helping as well. I was proud to hear their comments and knew that my main aim of making the crew a solid unit was working. Yes, the CSM and I could have been doing other work at the time, but the crew *esprit de corps* was more important for mission success. Lieutenant Bennett remarked that the [OC] had an accurate first hand account of what events were occurring in the AO as opposed to just gleaning information from patrol reports." In Afghanistan, the Coy actively pursued HUMINT sources and when successful passed them off to the HUMINT folks so they could exploit their potential information. I kept in contact with the local leaders much like my soldiers did so that missteps did not occur.

Another leadership challenge was working with coalition soldiers. Tasked as part of the Brigade QRF, the company formed the HQ element, as well as providing one platoon. The French and the Germans provided the remaining platoons. Initial problems encountered were due to communication limitations and the lack of uniform SOPs. After being tasked, I reported to the rendezvous location and waited for the other elements to arrive. Upon receiving orders from Brigade I drafted an exercise outline so that we could all practice joint responses to incidents. As well, I issued a modified set of SOPs that I used in the company so that everyone would be on the same sheet of music if were called upon to respond to an incident. However, one of the biggest barriers was communications. That was even with the addition of a Canadian signaler attached to each of the other coalition HQ elements.

At one time, I radioed the German platoon commander and told him to report to my location – only himself. Well… much to my surprise, he ended up bringing his whole platoon. Another major problem that occurred was that every nation would have a different mandate on where they are or are not allowed to meet. For example, some may not be able to travel into another nation's AO. The French, for one, had certain limitations that I only discovered when they told me they would not be participating in the nighttime exercise.

Throughout my time in Afghanistan, I endeavored to set the tempo, establish priorities such as intelligence gathering, develop HUMINT contacts, distribute aid in the hopes of getting added security, and winning the trust of the locals. I worked hard at guiding my direct subordinates so that they would glean aspects of my knowledge and character, and become more professional in their duties. However, my overarching aim besides all the others was to ensure our force protection. That was accomplished by building a strong team who was confident when given any task – a team that had confidence in their leaders, whether at the Section, Platoon, Company or even Battalion level.

ENDNOTES

1   Capt Kris Reeves started the tour as a Lt then was accelerated promoted to Capt for the latter half of the tour.

2   The Jowz valley was a Russian name for the valley, on our maps, where 3RCR suffered their first casualties.

CHAPTER 10

"WHERE THE WILLINGNESS IS GREAT...": LEADERSHIP LESSONS ABOARD THE *HMCS CHARLOTTETOWN* - OPERATION APOLLO

Lieutenant-Commander Ian Anderson

In October 2001, *Her Majesty's Canadian Ship (HMCS) Charlottetown* deployed on Operation (Op) Apollo with the Canadian Task Group that was sent as part of Canada's initial response to the American Global War on Terrorism. I was fortunate to be a member of the ship's crew for that deployment, and as a result, have taken up the challenge of sharing my experiences in an effort to provide potential lessons to others who may find themselves in similar situations.

Onboard the *HMCS Charlottetown*, I was one of the ship's three Operations Room Officers (ORO). The ORO qualification, the last level of occupational training for Maritime Surface and Subsurface (MARS) officers, comes after attending a year long course that involves classroom instruction, training in operations room simulators and a live assessment phase over a two-week period at sea. Upon completion of the course, officers join a ship where they assume the traditional title of either the Operations Officer or the Weapons Officer. These two officers stand watches in the operations room and are responsible for the effective execution of the mission, as well as for the conduct of their subordinate personnel on their watch.

The third officer in the operations room is the Combat Officer, who heads the entire Combat Department, which is comprised of all the Naval Operations Trades and the MARS Officers. The Combat Officer is an experienced individual who has normally acted as either the Operations Officer or Weapons Officer on the respective ship for six months to a year and who has assumed the senior position upon the posting-out (departure) of the previous Combat Officer. In my case, I was the Weapons Officer for the first year and a half of my time on *Charlottetown* and assumed the position of Combat Officer mid-way through Op Apollo.

Within the MARS community, we jokingly brag that "we like to eat our young." In essence, that is simply another way of saying that we have high standards and high expectations of junior officers as they progress through their training. While those junior officers may feel that they are being "ridden hard" what is actually at play is an ingrained practice of more senior experienced MARS officers teaching the next generation. As such, what follows is what I would tell those junior officers if we were sitting in the Wardroom of a ship discussing leadership.

SETTING THE STAGE

My tour on the *Charlottetown* was busy and during my two year posting I was either deployed or at sea and away from Halifax on training for approximately 15 of the 24 months. When I joined the ship, the focus of our efforts was to prepare to deploy with the United States Ship (USS) *Harry Truman* Carrier Battle Group in early 2001 for Op Augmentation. This meant a number of liaison visits to the *Truman's* base in Norfolk, Virginia, over the fall of 2000, as well as a major exercise that was the final step in the deployment work-up for the Battle Group. HMCS *Charlottetown* left Halifax in mid-January 2001, and after joining up with several other United States Navy (USN) ships, transited across the Atlantic to the Mediterranean where we spent several months training before moving through the Suez Canal and into the Arabian Gulf. The deployment proved to be very busy. At one period, for six days, the *Charlottetown* was the only ship off of the coast of Iraq in the Arabian Gulf enforcing United Nations Security Council Resolutions (UNSCR), specifically the exportation of oil in return for the import of humanitarian material. After a relatively uneventful but fulfilling tour, we arrived home in Halifax on 1 July 2001.

Once home, *Charlottetown's* crew commenced post deployment and summer leave. When we all returned to work in September following the Labour Day weekend we re-adjusted our focus to upcoming local fleet exercises and all the normal activities that come with being back in the Fleet. Our schedule was fairly light for the next year and I watched as classmates from my ORO course who had not been all that active for the first year of their posting start to get busy. After our ORO course, we all expected that at the end of our respective two-year postings, we would all come away with more or less the same amount of sea time and experience.

By 11 September, most of the crew of *Charlottetown* had barely begun to get back into their routines. As with most people, I can vividly remember where I was when I first heard what happened. I was in my cabin doing paperwork when someone called down the passageway from the Wardroom to say that a plane had crashed into one of the towers of the World Trade Centre in New York. For the next several hours we were all transfixed in front of the television as the events of that day played out.

Even in the immediate aftermath of the attacks, a lot of us had a sense Canada would, in some way, play a part in the inevitable response. At Maritime Forces Atlantic (MARLANT) Headquarters (HQ), the Plans and Operations Staffs went into contingency planning mode and within 36 hours had completed the Operational Planning Process (OPP) and developed a number of courses of action should the Government of Canada decide to send military forces. Despite what I am sure was the best efforts of the planning staff to keep their cards close to their chests, my cabin mate and I stumbled onto the news that *Charlottetown* was being considered as part of the Naval contribution. It was happenstance, when we bumped into a Chief Petty Officer who had been the second-in-command of a boarding party I had commanded on another ship. "*Charlottetown*, eh" he said. "I guess you are gearing up to head off again!" When he saw our surprised looks he realized that he might have let the cat out of the bag. He quickly excused himself by mumbling something about running late for a meeting and made his escape.

"Great," grumbled my cabin mate, "this is how it always starts." He and I headed for MARLANT HQ, confirmed that we were in the mix of options and subsequently attended the full decision brief to the Commander MARLANT at the end of the week. Then we waited.

When Prime Minister Jean Chrétien came back from Washington D.C. a week or so later and announced that our military assistance would not be required after all, I allowed myself a sigh of relief and re-focused on other issues. On 7 October 2001, I was working in my shed on a play table for my then one-and-a-half-year-old son when the CBC cut into its regular program to broadcast President George Bush's statement outlining the commencement of US forces attacking targets in Afghanistan. When the CBC announcer said that the Prime Minister would address the country in an hour, I cleaned up, went inside and waited for what I was pretty sure was the first indication that I would be deploying. As the Prime Minister announced that he had directed that "certain elements" of the Canadian Forces (CF) deploy, I knew that *HMCS Charlottetown* would be one of those elements. About an hour later, ten minutes before I sat down to what proved to be a completely tasteless Thanksgiving meal with my wife and her parents, my assumptions were confirmed when my Captain called to tell me that we were recalled and would sail in ten days.

Despite expecting the news, I was still a little shocked by it. Unfortunately, my reaction was to stand there with a dumb grin on my face as I told my wife the news. As she has reminded me several times since, this was not necessarily the best reaction to this kind of news – call that a pre-deployment lesson learned.

GETTING READY

The ten days prior to deploying were a blur. We lined up for the Departure Action Group (DAG) process, queued for passport pictures and additional kit and, where possible, spent as much time as we could with our families. Luckily, a lot of the preparations were very straightforward for the *Charlottetown*. We had barely been home for three months and many of the things that need to be done before a ship sails were already in place, with the exception of various stores and provisions. While quite a number of the junior non-commissioned members (NCMs) were newly arrived following the annual posting season, the command team (i.e. almost all the Heads of Departments and a large portion of the Chief and Petty Officers) had completed the Op Augmentation deployment. This, at least, meant that there was stability in the senior leadership. It also meant that the experience level of those senior NCMs and officers allowed us to prepare for the deployment with, perhaps, more ease that the other two ships who sailed as part of the Task Group.

The Task Group consisted of *HMCS Charlottetown*, *Iroquois* and *Preserver* and sailed from Halifax on 17 October 2001 amidst a great deal of pomp and ceremony. Over the next three weeks, the Task Group conducted combat enhancement training and, once in the Mediterranean Sea, spent time in Gibraltar and Souda Bay as well as the Greek island of Crete to complete final maintenance requirements before we proceeded through the Suez Canal. Similar to the days immediately preceding our departure from Halifax, a lot of this time was a blur but it was an important time as we worked hard to bring the ship to a high level of operational capability.

Onboard the *Charlottetown*, crossing the physical line represented by the Suez Canal marked a crossing of a psychological line. Up to that point everything that we had done was to prepare ourselves for working in a part of the world where there was a realistic threat. Once we crossed into the Red Sea everything was "for real" and an important part of our jobs as leaders was to make sure that our sailors understood that we were now in a place where people could hurt us (a point always brought home when you pass by Aden, in Yemen, where the *USS Cole* was attacked causing tremendous damage and numerous fatalities). It escaped no-one that we were undertaking a serious business. In terms of this particular operation, exiting from the southern terminus of the Suez Canal was also where the hard work of leadership began.

OPERATION APOLLO

Long deployments are hard. Yes, they have their professional challenges, many of which are very rewarding, and most certainly they can be a lot of fun. However, there are so many issues at play that can make them difficult undertakings for every single member of the ship's company. For this reason, it is vital as a leader to be aware of the complexities of life and how they are going to either affect individuals or groups. There are times when motivating people is going to be simple and there are times when you will struggle to try and explain to your sailors why they are doing some activity which, even to you, appears to be pointless. Nonetheless, as a leader you must maintain a consistent approach to how you lead your people regardless of the task or mission. Always explain the situation the best you can – but you must remain loyal to the chain command in the same manner that you remain loyal to your subordinates. It undermines their confidence and respect in both you and your superiors if denigrate decisions or direction from your superiors.

For *Charlottetown*, Op Apollo was a difficult deployment for a couple of reasons. Primarily, when ships return from national deployments (i.e. national being those directed and commanded by the Deputy Chief of the Defence Staff (DCDS), in essence normally an overseas operational deployment as opposed to a training exercise directed by a coastal commander – e.g. Commander MARLANT or MARPAC), they normally enter a period where the crew is protected from embarking on another major deployment for a period of six months. However, if required, as it was in this case, that six month "no touch" period can be waived.

Approximately 65 percent of the crew had been on Op Augmentation so Apollo represented the second major deployment away from home and families within a one-year period.

Another difficulty was the fact that once *Charlottetown* departed Souda Bay in early November, we remained at sea for 74 days! At the time, that represented a new record for a Canadian warship, at least in living memory and, anecdotally, it was thought that even during the Second World War the busy convoy escort ships had not achieved straight sea days of that duration. For those of you not familiar with watch rotations a sea, we maintained a 1-in-2 system that meant that at any time half of the ship's company was on watch. In the operations room we stood 12 hours worth of watches per day: five hours on, five hours off, seven hours on, seven hours off. My watch had the long middle watch, or long mids, from 0030-0730. The 1-in-2 watch system is only meant to be followed for two to three weeks after which it is understood that people begin to seriously tire. We maintained this pace for two and a half months. It was both physically and mentally draining.

There was also an additional element that made the deployment difficult for most of the ship's crew - that was a lack of communication, specifically the lack of information on what exactly our mission was, or would be. When we deployed from Halifax, we left with only a vague idea of what it was we were going to do once we got to the area of responsibility. This uncertainty remained for almost a month and it was not until we were well into the northern Indian Ocean that our final tasking was determined. That made it difficult to focus both our teams and ourselves.

Furthermore, setting a record by remaining at sea for 74 days straight might seem appealing to some but it made no sense to many us. While arguably our operational tempo protecting USN Amphibious Ready Group ships along the south coast of Pakistan could be described as largely sedate, it was still physically and mentally taxing. The other OROs and I failed to understand why, considering the overwhelming number of coalition warships in the area, a better rotation between patrols at sea and crew rest alongside could not be established. Although I am certain that there was a reason for the longevity of our patrol, I do not think that even our Captain fully understood the logic.

Unfortunately, the Canadian Staff commanding our Task Group never gave us an explanation. I am not sure if someone was afraid to simply tell us that we were deemed essential, or that there was no other way of balancing out our forces. Nonetheless, the lack of communication on this issue was frustrating for all of us. From this situation I think one can derive an important lesson: as a leader you cannot be afraid to tell people things that they do not want to hear. I think that people are far more resilient than we give them credit for and will carry on with the job even in the face of bad news. But, they want to know. Nothing is worse than a vacuum of information. It causes anxiety, frustration and rumours.

As I look back on Op Apollo with a couple of years of hindsight, I am not certain that I learned anything new about my own style of leadership. Rather, as I have outlined above, the operation presented its own sets of challenges that required actions by me in my leadership position and reinforced what I believed in terms of leadership. In any case, I will address my observations on leadership under the categories of my sailors, myself, and my boss

MY SAILORS

The primary lesson that stands out in my dealings with the sailors in my department, which, as the Combat Officer, numbered 75 people, is the importance of communication. Early on in the deployment, I began to get a lot of questions from the sailors on my watch about what we were doing or what was going to happen next. I always answered the best that I could. I would answer those questions one on one. As a normal part of standing watch in the operations room, the Combat Officer will periodically have everyone take their headsets off and give a quick situational report on whatever is going on. For example, if we were doing an anti-submarine exercise, I would summarize all the information we had about the location of the submarine and spell out what we were going to do next.

After a while, when enough sailors approached me with questions about the ship's activities and program it seemed that periodic big picture Situation Reports (SITREPs) were also required. After consulting with the operations room supervisor, we agreed that once a week we would get everyone from the Watch into the operations room and I would tell them what I knew and, just as importantly, what I did not know. I found these sessions to be very useful. They allowed me to regularly see everyone on the Watch including sailors who worked in the communications control room one deck above me (but who were responsible to me) and many of the officers of the Watch. I used these meetings, which normally lasted about 20 minutes, to review what we had been up to over the past week and acknowledge both overall and individual performances. We also looked ahead and, as our time at sea stretched on, often discussed when we were going to get a port visit and where that might be.

Again, if I did not know the answer, or knew that a port visit was not even on the horizon, I was honest with them. I also tried to keep the meetings as light-hearted as I could and usually ended them by soliciting the best rumour going around the ship about our program. Because we were at sea over the Christmas holiday period, these meetings were also an opportunity to wish everyone the best of the season. On New Year's Eve, although I could not buy them all a drink, I was at least to bring in a couple of cases of Canada Dry – the champagne of Ginger Ale!

In the end, these meetings were critical because they were another method to keep communications flowing. The passage of information is always important to everyone, particularly on operations. Whatever you as a leader can do to promote this will pay great dividends. People naturally want to know what will affect their future. Some handle uncertainty better than others. However, by passing on information as accurately and often as possible, a leader generates trust, credibility and respect. And equally important, the leader helps to minimize angst, fear and rumours.

MYSELF

It might seem a bit odd that I would talk about "me" in terms of leadership as one generally associates a certain sense of selflessness with leaders. Generally a leader makes sure their people are taken care of before looking after themselves. While this is a good guideline, I think that you have to remember that if you do not take care of yourself you will eventually become useless to your people. What does this mean?

I have mentioned several times that the 74 days at sea was both mentally and physically taxing. Days would become an endless repetition and after awhile a certain degree of monotony set in – much like the film "Groundhog Day" where an individual relived one day over and over again. One could very easily succumb to this monotony and become less effective. This is what started to happen to me early on during this period. At one point, I felt a physical malaise and went to see our physician's assistant complaining of a headache that would simply not go away. He took one look at me and in his normal "call it like it is" style asked me when I last saw sunshine. When I could not remember – I think it had been a week – he pointedly told me to stop being an idiot and get outside the ship for some sun and fresh air. As he put it, "You guys get a couple of gold bars on your shoulders and think that it makes you indestructible. You are no different than the rest of us." I took his point.

Following my encounter with the "Doc" I began to change my routine to include some time outside in the fresh air as well as some physical activity. Although it cut into the amount of sleep I was getting, I began to use the ship's treadmill and exercise bikes and I joined a fitness challenge that one of the sailors had started. I also took a little more time to write in a journal I had started at the beginning of the trip and downloaded a daily crossword that I would do just before I headed to bed. The end result was that I felt better. More importantly, I was able to continue to do my job with less likelihood that I was going to be irritable when on Watch, which would have negatively impacted the way my Watch performed. The lesson is that part of leadership is making sure you look after yourself in addition to your sailors. This directly affects how you are able to do your job, which of course has a direct effect on your subordinates.

MY BOSS

As I stated earlier, there was one area where I did learn a valuable lesson – sometimes you need to look after your boss. Your boss, whether you consider that to be your immediate supervisor or your Commanding Officer, feels all the same pressures that you do with the main difference being that they have more experience dealing with those pressures. In my case, I am talking about my Captain. For those of you who have never sat in the Captain's cabin I can assure you that the constant demands of command are taxing on anyone. There is never any rest for these senior officers who have to make decisions and respond to situations around the clock. And yet, as the physician's assistant pointed out, Captains are not indestructible (although some of them might feel differently). They are human, miss their families every bit as the rest of us, and ride the emotional roller coaster called a "deployment" like everyone else. Sometimes, they need a chance to vent their frustrations and, in the right circumstances, you can provide a sympathetic ear.

The Captain of the *Charlottetown* was an excellent officer and I very much enjoyed sailing with him. He knew everyone in the ship's company by name, made a point of walking through the ship every day and would often simply appear in an office or space where people were working and sit down and chat with them. He was always outgoing and positive about what we were doing and this demeanour went over very well with the sailors.

Op Apollo was the fourth time that he had deployed to the Gulf area in five years. In fact, he had had a high operational tempo for most of his career. When we returned from our US Carrier Battle Group deployment I think that he, like the rest of us, had looked forward to a slower tempo in his last year as a ship's Captain. To deploy again so suddenly was no easier for him than the rest of us and, like everyone else, he sometimes needed to vent his frustrations.

As the deployment progressed, a certain pattern developed where the Executive Officer and I would appear at the Captain's door around 1000 hours. We would be invited in, offered a cup of coffee and would discuss the messages that had come in overnight and the schedule for the next several days. It was during these coffee meetings that the Captain would do his venting and we would quietly listen. Once coffee and business was done, the Captain was able to continue his day with his normal positive outlook and he could leave his cabin with his "game face" on. What was said in the Captain's cabin stayed in the Captain's cabin and, while we were not able to solve all of the world's problems over a cup of really good coffee, the end result was that he felt better.

Now, this might not work in every situation. However, we always say that as a leader your loyalty goes in two directions: loyalty to your sailors and loyalty to your Captain. I would suggest that part of that loyalty is sensing when your "boss" needs some support even if that simply means giving him the opportunity to vent.

CONCLUSION

There is only one final point I wish to make about leadership and it comes from a 1960s Navy publication titled, *Guide to the Divisional System of the Royal Canadian Navy*. In addition to being full of what would now be considered politically incorrect cartoons, each chapter started with a quote from a wide variety of sources. My favourite quote, taken from Machiavelli, is fitting as a closing note as it sums up how one should approach their responsibilities as a leader: "Where the willingness is great, the difficulties cannot be great." In the end, a leader sets the tone. If you strive to be a professional in all you do, and if you sincerely care about those you work with – regardless of the challenges, you and those you serve with will persevere.

CHAPTER 11

OPERATIONAL READINESS – OPERATION APOLLO

A HELICOPTER AIR DETACHMENT COMMANDER'S PERSPECTIVE

Major Larry McCurdy

This chapter is first and foremost a story based on, and supported by, memories and experiences, mostly relating to Op Apollo, but not surprisingly filtered through 25 years of flying experience. My intent is not to chronologically recite events, as I suspect that some dates quoted herein are more approximations than fact, but rather to highlight challenges that I believe are common to contemporary operations. One example is the cultural differences between environments (i.e. Navy, Army and Air Force) that defy the comprehension of the uninitiated. Another, is the sustained operational tempo in excess of supportable resources; and a third is the subtle transition from pilot's discretion to blind adherence to 1 Canadian Air Division (CAD) orders that belies an outward appearance of wisdom and experience.

My intent, if not personal motivation, for taking the time to thoughtfully put four fingers to keyboard, is not to cast blame or take credit, but to inspire critical thinking in those who may be in a position to influence future operational environments and to assist those who will find themselves in the complex world of operations. It is also an effort to make a case for ensuring that the decisions and responsibilities incumbent on pilots who fly the actual missions remain with them and in the respective cockpit where they belong, rather than in the operations room of some geographically displaced headquarters. Instant global communications should never supplant command responsibility (or accountability) at any level, but particularly not in the cockpit.

This preamble will become self-evident soon enough. However, initially it is important to set the scene. Op Apollo was essentially a blockade of the Arabian Gulf area to prevent terrorists, and / or their supporters, from distributing arms and infiltrating personnel throughout the region. To assist with this task, the Canadian Sea King helicopters deployed to the region were fitted with surveillance and self-defence equipment to discourage terrorists in small vessels from conducting possible attacks against Allied surface vessels enforcing the blockade.

As such, in early March 2003, HMCS *Fredericton*, with her integral Sea King helicopter onboard, slipped from her jetty in Halifax and commenced the three-week journey to the Straits of Hormuz. This fact may not have been particularly noteworthy, except for the string of events and misadventures that preceded the departure. This chapter is an attempt to place those events into context and to describe the leadership challenges that faced a diverse collection of airmen in support of naval operations.

BACKGROUND

It is important to first understand that the Sea King community is somewhat abnormal. Our history and association link more closely to the Navy than the Air Force, yet the perception remains that we are not true members of either organization. The history behind this unfortunate fact is buried with the Fleet Air Arm and the dissolution of the Maritime Air Group Headquarters (MAG HQ), and would require volumes to discuss properly. For the purposes of this work, therefore, I will base the statement solely on my 25 years of association with the Maritime Helicopter environment. The ultimate result was that the Helicopter Air Detachment (HELAIRDET) personnel of Roto III (and their families) had a price to pay for the differences between the "we'll figure it out on the way" approach of the senior service (i.e. Navy), and the more controlled methodical 30-day pre-deployment training requirement attitude of its younger sibling (i.e. Air Force).

This, however, was not the last, nor the most critical leadership challenge attributable to a fundamental difference in culture between the Air Force and the Navy. The Air Force is a technology-based, reactive and rapidly deployable organization, that if need be, can take a combat-ready force into theatre within days. Unfortunately, maintaining combat readiness requires regular dedicated flying training hours, which places unsupportable demands upon two increasingly sparse resources: operations and maintenance (O&M) budgets and capital budgets. The reason for the former, obviously, is that gas, spare parts and personnel required for training, cost money that the Air Force did not have. Less obvious is the impact of an increased flying rate, required for maximum readiness, upon the life cycle of the fleet of aircraft and the capital requirements of accelerated air fleet replacements.

Downsizing, right sizing, restructuring and business planning are all colloquialisms for finding a way to meet operational commitments within available resources, and for the Air Force this has translated into maintainable levels of readiness. Fighter aircrew at reduced states of readiness may train just enough to preserve core skills, and then, given sufficient warning, they would ramp up the training specific to the upcoming mission, and deploy on time, with the right tools for the job. It all makes perfect business sense, but it is not worth a plug nickel if the mission changes significantly, as is sometimes the case.[1] Nevertheless, for reasons of economics and flight safety, the Air Force rigidly requires a minimum of 30 days notice of deployment in order to be able to provide mission-specific combat ready crews in support of an operation.

The Navy, by way of comparison, has taken a different tack on the same issue. It has been said, albeit incorrectly, that Seamanship is just Airmanship at twelve knots. However, when travelling at 500 Knots per hour, pre-deployment preparation is mission critical, whereas, at 12 knots per hour you have lots of time to consider and train en route. Furthermore, preparing and supplying the ship takes time, but you can also arrange for additional deliveries at numerous ports-of-call. Equipment must be repaired and maintained, but that can normally be done during the 2-6 week transit period to the latest trouble spot. Operational training standards must be maintained (or achieved), but that is best done while underway, where normal office hours do not apply. Therefore, it becomes obvious why the Navy's philosophical approach is diametrically opposed to the Air Force's "get ready, then go" culture. The net result is that in the cross-cultural struggle, there was a strong possibility that the Sea King could be left in Canadian Forces Base (CFB) Shearwater to complete the Air Force pre-deployment requirements, while its floating airport sailed into harms way alone.[2]

Cultural issues aside, the most critical leadership challenge of ROTO III was the inexperience of the Sea King aircrew in general. This challenge will be the focus of this chapter, specifically two issues: a. the impact of the 1997 decision of the Minister of National Defence (MND) requiring all officers to have an undergraduate degree and its effect on the demographic (and hence experience) of 423 Maritime Helicopter (MH) Squadron[3]; and b. the culture of the higher headquarters that centres on attention to detailed regulation rather than training and devolved responsibility. In the end, I have found that neither age nor rank equates to experience in the current context, and that there is an alarming tendency amongst inexperienced aircrew to look to regulations for a solution to a situation where in the past common sense and judgement were expected.

OPERATIONAL READINESS

By the fall of 2002, 423 MH Squadron was under the microscope for shortfalls in operational readiness, as defined by 1 CAD Orders, and as evaluated by the Maritime Helicopter Standards and Evaluation Team (MH SET). I have no intention, despite unshakable faith in my old Squadron, of disputing the findings of the MH SET, but it must be pointed out that audits like those conducted by 1 CAD HQ staff amount to an assessment of administrative procedures, rather than of true operational capabilities. I can say this with conviction since I was once a member of the now-defunct MAG HQ Maritime Air Standards Team (MAST), which was then responsible for conducting identical audits.

1 CAD Orders require that each crewmember fly a specified number of hours and track specific manoeuvres on a monthly and rolling quarterly basis.[4] Aside from a crew commander's inherent requirement to train and evaluate the crew, there is no stated requirement to fly any tracked manoeuvre to a pre-established standard. This raises the perennial debate of currency versus proficiency in terms of how exactly does one define operational readiness. It also highlights my argument that the squadron's only deficiency was its ability to quantify its readiness, and that arguably is what staff officers are for. I would still gladly fly a Sea King on the most challenging missions with any of my former squadron-mates, even though I might not ask all of them to write a memorandum.

I arrived into this environment as a "retread" co-pilot, assigned to *HMCS Iroquois* helicopter air detachment. Within three months, I had suffered through the complete upgrading process, as mandated by 1 CAD, for Maritime Helicopter Captain (MHC) and Maritime Helicopter Crew

Commander (MHCC) qualifications. Most noteworthy, at this point was the increasing delta between what a Sea King pilot had to know, and what a Sea King pilot actually did operationally. Personal experience from the distant past made me a believer in the requirement to train as you fight, but what I saw was a dichotomy.

For training, a pilot had to have a detailed understanding of anti-submarine warfare (ASW), even though many MHCCs had never actually tracked a submerged submarine...ever. Aircrew were tested regularly on their knowledge of brevity code words for items like hostile submarine or ASW torpedoes, despite the fact that most had never carried a torpedo, much less dropped one. Air plans are pre-established tactics designed for rapid, accurate ASW employment of air and surface assets. These had to be committed to memory, despite the fact that since Somalia, the Sea King had been employed in more surface surveillance roles than virtually any other. For this role the Sea King was fitted with a 7.62 general purpose machine gun (GPMG), Forward Looking Infra-red (FLIR) missile approach warning equipment and CHAFF and Flare dispensers. These capabilities, which had become central to our employment, however, were not taught during conversion training because the tasks were not part of the classic operational mission of a maritime helicopter. Reality had not yet caught up to the conventional wisdom.

For Op Apollo, our mission was surveillance, and potentially interdiction of small terrorist vessels attacking High Value Units (HVU). Flying surveillance was not considered part of our combat readiness, except that it counted toward the monthly required flying time. As a result, the mission became one where a pilot could deploy to an active theatre, fly nothing but operational missions, and return home six months later and be considered less operationally ready than when he or she originally deployed. Certainly, if tested on brevity code words (as most communications in the Gulf were mechanically encrypted), or ASW tactics, the crew may be found to be sorely lacking. But does that really indicate an inability to do what Sea King helicopters really do?

HMCS Iroquois was scheduled to deploy on Op Apollo in June 2003. Six months prior, in January 2003, as a newly qualified MHCC, I was appointed as the ship's air detachment commander. My intention was to conduct team-building so that by the summer we would be a cohesive unit, fully qualified and operationally ready. At a glance it seemed that experience was not a problem. Myself aside, the other pilot MHCC although newly upgraded, was highly respected for his knowledge and skill. The average age of the aircrew was well over 30 years, and given five months to prepare, I expected that all the cards had been stacked in my favour. Despite the fact that the three pilots and two Air Navigators were all first-tour officers, most had been to the Gulf at least once, and for them, this should be old-hat. This assumption would come back to haunt me as the most potentially critical mistake of the deployment. Despite being blind to this eventuality at the start, my confidence was still short-lived.

During my get acquainted visit with the Captain of *HMCS Iroquois*, my hopes for a slow and easy transition back to operational life were shattered when he shared with me his suspicion that June was likely not going to be our deployment date after all. He speculated that sometime between then and early March could be chosen, and that we would accompany *HMCS Fredericton* on Roto III. The ship had an unknown timeframe to complete full workups, and due to the recent arrival of the HELAIRDET, air workups would have to be done as well. I believed it was achievable, but we needed to get to sea and work out the bugs. At least, I thought to myself, I had a Gulf-experienced HELAIRDET.

I returned to the squadron and suggested that the preparations should commence for a likely deployment in February. Given that all squadron members must maintain a current DAG (Departure Assistance Group) part-one (administration for operational deployments[5]) we decided to start on the part-two proceedings as soon as possible. We also had to look at an accelerated training schedule to include more crew flying hours, and the updating of mandatory pre-embarkation training. However, when word of a possible early deployment reached the Air Force, an unexpected response instantly brought our status of lost souls between two diametrically opposed and competing cultures. Our higher headquarters directed that we were not, repeat NOT, to begin any preparations for deployment until the Navy issued an official warning order, giving at least 30 days notice to deploy.

In the days that followed we inventoried our spare part "pack-ups," scheduled all of the DAG part-one updates, inspected the HELAIRDET spaces for required repairs and we waited for the official word to openly begin preparations. Ultimately, it was decided to switch our HELAIRDET for that of *HMCS Fredericton*, since that ship was already operationally ready. As such, my newly formed detachment would only have to complete air workups, and *HMCS Iroquois* would only require ship's workups. All around it was considered to be a more economical use of resources. My problems diminished because now I could concentrate exclusively on the training requirements of the aircrew…or so I assumed.

The first of the new wave of challenges came when the aircraft designated for our HELAIRDET was delayed in refit. We expected to have a week or two to fly off the rough edges and to team-build with the newly organized crews. Ultimately, and to our later dismay, time permitted only one hour of post-test flight shakedown. Amazingly, the first opportunity to fly as a dedicated crew came on embarkation day. Meanwhile, the DAG part-two process was to prove much more difficult than previously anticipated.

Once the warning order was issued, 1 CAD HQ required daily reports on the status of pre-embarkation training. The Navy, for their part was now concerned that the Helicopter would not be available for a timely departure. As the Detachment Commander, the perception that Big Brother was watching was unavoidable. We embarked twenty-eight days later, after dedicating virtually all of the available resources of 12 Wing to completing the overhaul of our assigned aircraft, and rearranging every possible training schedule to complete, without possible exception, all of the DAG requirements. Eight aircrew, and eleven technicians worked virtually every day, weekends and evening included, to complete escape and evasion training, Helo Firefighting training, range qualification (in the air and on the ground), NBCD (nuclear, biological, chemical defence) training, missile avoidance training, and all of the interviews and briefings required prior to embarkation. Most of the HELAIRDET had the opportunity to spend their last weekend at home, as part of the mandatory pre-embarkation leave, but we had not managed to fly a single dedicated crew proficiency training flight. Sea King 410 was test flown serviceable on the Thursday prior to departure.

THE CRASH OF SEA KING 401

In the middle of this frenzy of preparation, a MH aircrew from *HMCS Iroquois* experienced a catastrophic power loss while on work-ups. The helicopter crashed on deck, and was seriously damaged, luckily with only minor injuries to the crew. A new leadership challenge had presented itself when my entire MH detachment watched on national television as they craned the remains of Sea King 401 off the deck of *HMCS Iroquois*, knowing that but for the grace of 1 CAD that it could have been one of us in that wreck.

Fortunately for me, a common characteristic of Sea King aircrew is unshakable optimism. They took it upon themselves to reassure friends and family that accidents happen and that they were more than qualified to deal with any eventuality. Every single member of our HELAIRDET confirmed his willingness to continue flying, despite the crash, and the two ships, less one helicopter, departed Halifax together, as scheduled.

THE TRANSIT

Anyone associated with the Maritime Helicopter community must understand that hell hath no fury like the confluence of air work-ups and a following sea. During the eight-day transit between Halifax and Gibraltar, wind, rain and sea-state conspired to make deck-training evolutions almost impossible. Most events required deck motion limits of less than 3 degrees of pitch and 10 degrees of roll, and evaluating staff were vigilant to ensure that the limits were not exceeded. Mother Nature took care of the rest, by keeping over half of the ship's company, to include the HELAIRDET personnel, preoccupied with seasickness. We were well into the Mediterranean Sea before we could complete the required serials to the satisfaction of the evaluators, and be declared operationally ready for employment. By that time we had been given cause to regret the too-brief maintenance shakedown of our hurriedly refitted aircraft.

AIRCRAFT SERVICEABILITY

While still only halfway through the Mediterranean Sea, a vigilant technician noticed a small hole in the titanium firewall between the engine and the cabin. Upon closer inspection, it was discovered that the engine had been installed in such a way as to bring a fuel drain valve into intermittent contact with the firewall, due to vibration. Over time, even titanium suffers fatigue failure, and a small diameter hole appeared. An engine fuel leak, in conjunction with such a hole could have been disastrous.[6] Fortunately, the hole was discovered in the best possible circumstances. Unfortunately, we lacked the resources for local repair and we were grounded for an extended period.

Rather than allow idle minds to speculate on the condition of other key aircraft components, and risk having the aircrew and maintainers lose faith in the aircraft, I ordered a thorough post-periodic inspection of the entire aircraft. The results were both discouraging and redeeming; nine previously undetected major unserviceabilities were discovered, but in the end, the technicians, having taken ownership of the machine, were proud of their accomplishments and were uniformly willing to fly as crew. It was discovered that the overhaul facility at Shearwater had been overstretched to provide aircraft to the fleet since Roto 0. As memory serves, 13 separate deployments, most with helicopters on-board had ventured into the Gulf prior to our arrival. Overtime was commonplace and the pressure to deliver our aircraft on time became extreme when post-periodic maintenance required a dual engine change, a main gearbox change and major fuel cell repairs. Nevertheless, we had renewed confidence in aircraft reliability and a sense of accomplishment. Three weeks later we resumed flying operations.

OPERATIONAL FLYING AT LAST

Now in the Gulf and with all maintenance problems rectified we began flying the long-intended mission. Given the surveillance role, and the prevailing meteorological conditions, I had ordered the removal of all non-essential equipment. The SONAR and all related electronics were removed at a savings of over 500 pounds gross weight, which allowed for 30 minutes worth of extra fuel. With an original zero-fuel weight of 16,400 pounds, hovering out of ground effect was out of the question with less than an hour of fuel (plus reserves) on board. As such, the 30 minutes of extra fuel significantly improved our effectiveness. The Sea King had been originally designed to operate in the Atlantic Ocean with a density altitude (DA)[7] near zero and generally moderate winds to help reduce the power requirement. In the Gulf the prevailing DA was well over 4000 Feet above Sea Level (ASL), and typically zero wind, meaning the Sea King was power-limited in the extreme. Our first task was to adjust the aggressive aircrew to the new paradigm of power management and understanding the flight envelope.

This was the critical juncture of the deployment where I began to understand that age does not necessarily equate to experience, and not all experiences are created equal. Earlier missions had been scheduled as training flights, and the initial operational missions were consumed with allaying in-theatre jitters and generally becoming familiar with the environment. Now, as we settled into our new comfort zone, I began drilling the crew with emergency scenarios, and using the many transits to hone procedures and flying skills with critical systems secured. One day, the other MHCC enquired as to why I was doing crew training when the mission was only authorized for surveillance. He believed that I was conducting unauthorized training and was putting myself in a tenuous position in the event of an accident. What I was about to discover through a series of pointed questions was that on previous deployments, some crews had spent the entire deployment doing only tasked missions, which amounted to flying around, systems-on, predominantly in the daytime, without conducting even rudimentary crew training. The training value of such a flight is virtually nil and my shock was palpable.

Clearly, the MHCC, despite personal competence, had not been doing all that I had expected an MHCC to do, because he had been trained in an environment that blindly accepted rules and ideas without critical thought. The senior co-pilots were not as senior as I had assumed, because the hours in the logbook did not represent the experiences that I had been afforded at that same stage in my career. I recalled almost staggering out of the aircraft after yet another gruelling day of partial-panel hydraulics off engine failures at the hands of my tormentor, Lieutenant-Commander, United States Navy (USN) Brunson. I remembered Captain Joe Hincke pulling engines when I least expected (or wanted) it, then quietly chuckling as I tried to get us out of the pickle that my inexperience, poor judgement and overconfidence had allowed him to put us into. I also recollected thanking them silently on several occasions during my flying career. The people, now under my command, had been denied those experiences and it became my personal mission to rectify this dangerous and unsatisfactory training inadequacy. But fist I had to understand why intelligent, educated officers would think in such a regimented fashion.

Each of the officers on my Detachment were at least as educated, and in many cases more educated, than I was. Critical thinking should have been part of their culture. Most had attended the Royal Military College of Canada (RMC) and at least one was an RMC Engineer. I had enough intellectual horsepower in my Detachment to power the ship across the Atlantic. Still they were flawed, from an operational perspective.

MND 10

Under no circumstances would I ever suggest that it is a bad idea to have educated officers. I do believe, however, that there are different requirements for junior officers destined to learn how to fight a war with machines, than those for a staff officer. The simple truth is that the young are predominantly responsible for fighting wars, and the experienced use their knowledge to prepare the young to do better. As implied earlier, the decision to front-end load the education of our young officers, as supported in MND 10, has resulted in a five to seven year increase in the average age of front-line aircrew. Where in the past the simple fact of being a captain meant that you were a veteran of at least two major deployments is no longer the case. Many captains have not even qualified on their first operational aircraft.

A second truism is that a 27-year old father of two, thinks, acts and reacts entirely differently than does a recent graduate of high school and pilot training. It is my contention that education without experience is like drinking fine wine without taste buds – you can do it, but what's the point? The "Degree'd Officer Corps" with all its good intentions has changed the demographic of the operational squadrons from freethinking, experience hungry operators, to reserved, respectful unquestioning rule followers. Not a bad situation if you are an accounting firm, but deadly in a reactive war fighting scenario.

In response to what I believed to be a dangerous gap in experience and training, I directed that all missions were training missions, on a non-interference opportunity basis with the tasked operational mission. I subsequently scheduled flights, such that every pilot on HELAIRDET would have the opportunity to suffer from my instruction; first on the list was my MHCC. Again, the depth that orders had been engrained into operational thinking surprised me. While conducting a maintenance test flight *HMCS Fredericton* requested that we investigate a surface contact that was closing in on her on a steady bearing. While I altered course to investigate, my young MHCC was adamant that we were only authorized to do a test flight, and no other mission could be tasked until the aircraft was certified serviceable. I conceded that this was true in accordance with the rules, but given that we were in a war zone, sticking rigidly to that direction might just cost us our airport. Responsibility for our decision is why they give us rank and wings. We investigated the contact prior to landing, but it was clear to me that this paradigm shift was not going to occur overnight.

HOW DID WE GET HERE?

The loss of initiative and judgement by pilots and their servitude and blind adherence to directives and regulations that are clearly at odds with the reality of a complex and fast moving operational setting is troublesome. Yet, its not hard to understand the circumstances that brought us here. Firstly, command-level scrutiny is clearly obvious down to the unit level, such that a squadron major reports daily through the Wing, directly to 1 CAD. Perhaps the higher headquarters lacked confidence in the Wing to manage its own affairs, or perhaps earlier regimes were forced to respect a slower pace of information flow up and down the chain of command simply because technology did not afford the instant gratification that we enjoy today. Certainly, in this case, technology is a two-edged sword.

A second factor is the fact that Roto III occurred at the end of an extended period of high operational tempo, and the maintenance resources were stretched to capacity and beyond. Conceivably this was indicative of perceived pressure resulting from microscopic oversight, or more likely, it was suggestive of the "can-do" attitude common in the MH community. In either case, it was resource intensive and lapses in "combat readiness" bookkeeping may have diminished the confidence of auditing agencies - an understandable by-product, thereby prompting their over-involvement and oversight.

Finally, and most importantly, the matter of competent and respected aircrew who are more concerned with obeying a directive than using common sense and pilot discretion to judge when it might be appropriate to throw 1 CAD Orders in the drink raises concern. Falling back on simpler times, I recall that the predecessor of 1 CAD Orders (MAG Orders or MAGORDS) was a relatively thin document that set reasonable guidelines and expressly expected pilots to use their experience and judgement to determine the most effective course for mission accomplishment. This concept has been replaced by a mindset that tries to regulate every eventuality. More than a decade later, 1 CAD Orders have expanded to the extent that almost any scenario has been considered. Take as a case in point, the MAGORD requirement to wear an immersion suit for flight over water. When the water temperature was 13 degrees Celsius or more and the sum of the air temperature and water temperature was 31degrees or better, immersion suits were worn at the discretion of the aircraft captain. The 1 CAD version expands further to say, if the air temperature is between 10 degrees and 13 degrees, and the flight is conducted within a certain inexplicable range of land, and radio checks are conducted every 15 minutes, then immersions suits are not required. To further engrain the level of control exercised by higher headquarters, aircrew are annually required to recite the regulation verbatim on the MH SET exam. More weight is placed on a verbatim response to any question on the exam as opposed to a confirmation as to whether or not there is a clear understanding of what the regulation actually means.

For instance, my response to the above question is that as MHCC, my crew would always wear an immersion suit for sustained over-water flights unless the water temperature is over 15 degrees Celsius, because as a ship's diver, I understand the impact of cold-water egress and its consequences on survivability beyond initial impact. When I am not the designated MHCC, I would wear the immersion suit and let the MHCC decide for himself. My answer would be wrong for the purposes of the MH SET exam. Is it then surprising that the new generation of Sea King aircrew live and die by the book?

HOW DID I CHOOSE TO RESPOND?

It is an inescapable truism that change occurs. I could not reasonably expect to find the Maritime Helicopter environment exactly as I had left it almost a decade earlier. Nevertheless, the old axiom of not throwing the baby out with the bathwater holds true in this case. It is critical for the senior leadership to foster critical thinking at all levels of command, and never to blindly criticize a reasoned and reasonable decision, even when it does not work out exactly as intended. Such was my direction to the members of my HELAIRDET, by word and deed.

One of my best examples is a situation that had significant potential for disaster. As a part of crew training, my aircraft captain-qualified co-pilot was required to sign-out the aircraft as aircraft captain, despite the fact that I was in over-all command of the mission. On one particular flight, we were practicing mine disposal tactics using Explosive Ordinance Disposal (EOD) divers and live explosives. Without discussing the precise procedures, it is sufficient to say that the diver had a limited amount of time in which to plant the explosive and return to the helicopter. As described earlier, the Sea King was severely power limited in the Gulf environment, and this tactic demanded a protracted hover. The Sea King is also susceptible to false engine fire indications in conditions of high ambient temperatures, low wind and high torque.

In this instance, we had just put the diver in the water when the engine fire indicator illuminated. As a good co-pilot, I alerted the flying pilot, and he took action to put the aircraft in a safe regime of flight. Now, having established that the fire indication was of a spurious nature, we returned to the hover to recover the diver, who had set (and armed) the explosive and was swimming for recovery. Not unexpectedly, the fire indication returned as soon as we were established in the hover. I was comfortable under the circumstances remaining in the hover just long enough to recover our diver, but the aircraft captain is responsible for the safety of flight decisions and chose to fly away, temporarily leaving the diver stranded in the water. As MHCC I did not agree, as I am certain the diver did not, but I was forced to accept the decision of the person in whom I had placed the burden of responsibility. As a learning tool I later made him defend his decision to the diver and to me, but reinforced his right to make that decision as well as his responsibility for the outcome.

It would have been too easy to override his decision and, notwithstanding the fact that I had already calculated that there remained sufficient time to return and recover the diver, had I done so I would have possibly destroyed any motivation for taking command and making split-second decisions. Aside from spoiling his credibility with the crew, subsequent decisions would always have been preceded by a pause to see what I really wanted him to do. The concept that leaders are born and not developed is arguably supportable, but it is a certainty that leadership potential can be easily diminished, particularly in its infancy.

MOST EFFECTIVE LEADERSHIP PRINCIPLE

Overall, my detachment was motivated, disciplined and competent. There was no requirement to impose my will upon an unruly mob, nor to inspire the uninspired. In most cases by the time I recognized a requirement for action, one of my many talented members had already responded appropriately. The strengths of my staff, being many, were easily identifiable and willingness to allow them to exercise those talents made my task all the easier. Yet, leadership is required in every scenario, and my guiding principle for this calibre of individual was to understand the difference between occasions requiring firm direction and oversight, from those better served by allowing the potential for mistakes and the lessons that are inevitably learned from them.

LESSONS RELEARNED

At the end of the tour a number of lessons, that were relearned, became evident:

1. Train as you fight and test for understanding.

2. Make your quality assurance measures reflect true capability, rather than mathematically or logistically quantifiable sums. Operational readiness should mean your crews are able to fight your aircraft in whatever environment is required by the mission. It should not mean that you have flown 30 hours within the last 30 days, or that you can use a SONAR device that will be removed immediately upon arrival in theatre. Rather it should be based on performance as assessed by a qualified Standards Officer, as delegated by an accountable and responsible Commanding Officer.

3. Establish an operational culture guided by regulations, but not depen-dant upon unswerving recitation of chapter and verse so that education can be filtered through experience, instead of filtering experience through book learning. The danger of MND 10 as the sole means of offi-cer production is that we now have a generation of young officers who seem to think that every answer is found in a book, regulation or order, when in fact, life is rarely that simple – and war never is.

4. Encourage and promote common sense, while learning from mistakes (ideally those of others).

5. Expect thoughtful initiative, but demand accountability.

As a final word of advice, enjoy your time with the group you command, which is normally a diverse group of men and women who you will come to revere as family. I look back with pride at my experience aboard *HMCS*

Fredericton. I can say without fear of exaggeration that the ship's company (and in that I include the HELAIRDET) constituted the finest group of people with whom I have ever had the pleasure to serve.

ENDNOTES

1   Sea King helicopters were deployed to Somalia to provide ship to shore re-supply, but ended up doing reconnaissance missions day and night, armed with a light machine gun and night vision equipment. It was a learn-as-you-go operation.

2   *HMCS Iroquois,* after the pre-deployment training crash of CH-12401, departed for the Gulf without a replacement helicopter, which had to be shipped to theatre at a later date.

3   http://www.forces.gc.ca/site/minister/eng/pm/mndmilitary.html MND 10 - The directive that required an undergraduate degree as a prerequisite for commissioning (with the exception of Commissioning From the Ranks for selected Senior NCOs).

4   Specific manoeuvres are counted on a monthly or quarterly basis. For example, you must do at least one practice autorotation (this is the way you must land if both engines fail) every three months. For safety reasons, these must be practiced over a runway at a controlled airport. We did not have an airport to use for training while in theatre and therefore we were considered to be not operationally ready. You must also do a transition to the hover on instruments, an instrument recovery from the hover (called a freestream) and a myriad of other manoeuvres. A crew must only report which manoeuvres they practiced on any given flight, not how well or effectively it was accomplished; therefore, these tracked manoeuvres are called "Stats"…damned lies and statistics! A shortfall in stats results in that crew being removed from flying until the deficiency is corrected – somewhat akin to canceling leave until morale improves.

5   DAG – Departure Assistance Group. To most it is a form / process that must be completed before you can be cleared for deployment. It includes the completion of such administration as next of kin information, medical and dental checks, etc…The DAG part-two is normally completed just prior to an anticipated deployment, and requires more thorough scrutiny such as interviews by social workers or the Padre, completed wills and updating of insurance information.

6   In 1994, Sea King 425 was destroyed, and two pilots killed when fuel penetrated the cabin through a hole in the firewall, causing a serious in-flight fire.

7   Density altitude allows us to calculate the power required to hover at sea level, as temperature, pressure and humidity vary from ICAO Standard.

CONTRIBUTORS

Lieutenant-Commander **Ian Anderson** was the Combat Officer in *HMCS Charlottetown* and deployed on Op Apollo as part of the initial Canadian contribution to the war on terrorism. He is currently serving with Joint Task Force Atlantic as a Senior Staff Officer for Domestic Operations

Major **Tony Balasevicius** is an infantry officer and member of The Royal Canadian Regiment (RCR). He has held various platoon and company command positions in all three battalions of The RCR, as well as in the Canadian Airborne Regiment. He was also the DCO of 1 RCR in 2002-2004. He is currently a Directing Staff at the Department of Applied Military Science at RMC.

Lieutenant-Colonel **Dave J. Banks** is an infantry officer with 31 years of service: eight as a Reserve NCO and the remainder as an officer in the PPCLI. He is currently the senior officer, advanced military studies at the Canadian Forces College.

Lieutenant-Colonel **Howard G. Coombs** retired from full time service with the Canadian Forces in 2002. He is a graduate of the United States Army Command and General Staff College, where he was one of eleven students who earned the designation US Army Master Strategist in 2001, and the US Army School of Advanced Military Studies, which awarded his Master's degree. He is currently a doctoral candidate at Queen's University and the Commanding Officer of the Princess of Wales' Own Regiment in Kingston.

Colonel, Dr. **Bernd Horn** is the Director of the Canadian Forces Leadership Institute. He was the CO of 1 RCR (2001-2003); the OC 3 Commando, the Canadian Airborne Regiment (1993-1995); and the OC "B" Company, 1 RCR (1992-1993). He is also an Adjunct-Associate Professor of History at the Royal Military College of Canada.

Major **Larry McCurdy**, enrolled in 1979 and received his pilot's wings in 1981. He commanded the HELAIRDET, *HMCS Fredericton* on Op Apollo, Roto 3 from March to August 2003. He is currently the SSO Selection CFRG HQ Borden.

Lieutenant-Colonel **Ian MacVicar** is an Artillery officer who has held staff and command positions in 4 CMBG, SSF, 2 CMBG, and the DCDS Group; most recently as the first Commanding Officer of the CF Joint NBCD Company. He holds a BA (Honours) from Acadia University, a MA in Conflict Analysis from Carleton University, and a MA of Defence Studies from RMC. He was awarded the CDS and DCDS Commendations for leadership in arms control verification and DART operations.

Major **Kevin Caldwell** enrolled in the CF in 1985, and he has commanded from platoon to company level. He has served in 2 RCR (mechanized infantry bn), in 3 Commando, the Canadian Airborne Regiment, and in 3 RCR (para coy, light infantry bn), and in 1 RCR (LAV infantry battalion). He is currently DNBCD 2-5 Force Protection at NDHQ.

Major **Tom M. Mykytiuk** was OC "N" Coy from April 2003 to July 2004. He has served on a number of UN and NATO missions with the First, Second and Third Battalions of The Royal Canadian Regiment. He is currently the Chief Instructor at Land Forces Western Area Training Centre.

Major **Neil Tabbenor** joined the regular force as a Direct Entry Officer in 1987. He deployed on Op Apollo as the Long Range Patrol Detachment Maintenance Flight Commander for Roto 0. He is currently the CP-140 System Engineering Officer at NDHQ.

Colonel **Jonathan Vance** is an infantry officer (The RCR) and has commanded from platoon to battalion level. He has completed the UK Combined Arms Tactics Course, CLFCSC, CFCSC and the Advanced Military Studies Course. He holds a BA in Military and Strategic Studies and a MA in War Studies. Colonel Vance is currently employed as Chief of Staff Land Forces Central Area.

GLOSSARY
OF ABBREVIATIONS AND ACRONYMS

Admin	Administration
ADM PA	Associate Deputy Minister Public Affairs
AEO	Aircraft Engineering Officer
AEPM	Aerospace Project Management
AERE	Aerospace Engineer
AFM	Air Flow Multiplier
AGL	Above Ground Level
AIMP	Aurora Incremental Modernisation Project
AMF	Afghan Militia Forces
ANA	Afghan National Army
APC	Armoured Personnel Carrier
AO	Area of Operations
AT	Anti Tank
ATI	Access to Information Act
ASL	Above Sea Level
ASO	Acoustic Sensor Operators
ASW	Anti Submarine Warfare
AVGP	Armoured Vehicle General Purpose
AWOL	Absence Without Official Leave
BBC	British Broadcasting Corporation
BG	Battle Group
BH	Bosnia-Hercegovina
BHQ	Battalion Headquarters
BMD	Ballistic Missile Defence
Bn	Battalion
BTE	Brigade Training Event
C4ISR	Command, Control, Communications, Computers, Intelligence, Surveillance and Reconnaissance
CAD	Canadian Air Division
CANBAT	Canadian Battalion
CBC	Canadian Broadcasting Corporation
CC	Corrosion Controls
CDS	Chief of the Defence Staff

CEF	Canadian Expeditionary Force
CENTCOM	Central Command
CER	Combat Engineer Regiment
CF	Canadian Forces
CFE	Canadian Forces Europe
CFHQ	Canadian Forces Headquarters
CFLI	Canadian Forces Leadership Institute
CID	Critical Incident Debriefing
CIDA	Canadian International Development Agency
CIMIC	Civilian Military Cooperation
CISS	Canadian Institute of Strategic Studies
CMBG	Canadian Mechanized Brigade Group
CMO	Chief Military Observer
CMS	Chief of the Maritime Staff
CNN	Cable News Network
CO	Commanding Officer
COP	Concept of Operations
CP	Canadian Press or Command Post (context dependent)
CQ	Company Quartermaster
CRS	Chief of Review Services
CSM	Company Sergeant Major
CTC	Combat Training Centre
CTF	Canadian Task Force
DAG	Departure Assistance Group
DART	Disaster Assistance Response Team
DCBA	Director Compensation Benefits Administration
DCDS	Deputy Chief of the Defence Staff
DCO	Deputy Commanding Officer
DGPA	Director General Public Affairs
DND	Department of National Defence
DPRE	Displaced Persons, Refugees and Evacuees
EOD	Explosive Ordinance Disposal
FLIR	Forward Looking Infrared Radar
FP	Force Protection
GDP	Gross Domestic Product
GPS	Global Positioning System

HDZ	*Hrvatska Demokratska Zyednica*
HELAIRDET	Helicopter Air Detachment
HF	High Frequency
HLVW	Heavy Lift Vehicle Wheeled
HN	Host Nation
HQ	Headquarters
HUMINT	Human Intelligence
HUMVEE	High-Mobility, Multipurpose Wheeled Vehicle
HVO	*Hrvatsko Vijece Odbrane*
HVU	High Value Units
IC	International Community
ICG	International Crisis Group
ICTY	International War Crimes Tribunal for the Former Yugoslavia
IED	Improvised Explosive Device
IFOR	Intervention Force
IO	International Organizations
ISAF	International Security Assistance Force
ITI	Impact Teams International
JAG	Judge Advocate General
JCO	Joint Commission Observers
JTF-CAM	Joint Task Force – Central America
JNA	Yugoslav People's Army
LAV	Light Armoured Vehicle
LFWA	Land Forces Western Area
LIO	Leadership Interdiction Operations
Log	Logistics
LRP	Long Range Patrol
LSVW	Light Support Vehicle Wheeled
MAG HQ	Maritime Air Group Headquarters
Maint O	Maintenance Officer
MARLANT	Maritime Forces Atlantic
MARPAC	Martime Forces Pacific
MAST	Maritime Air Standards Team
MHCC	Maritime Helicopter Crew Commander
MH SET	Maritime Helicopter Standards and Evaluation Team

MND	Minister of National Defence
MND (SW)	Multinational Division (Southwest)
MP	Member of Parliament or Military Police (context determines)
MRP	Maritime Recognized Picture
MSF	*Medcins Sans Frontiere*
MTC	Militia Training Centre
NASO	Non-Acoustic Sensor Operators
NATO	North Atlantic Treaty Organization
NAVCOM	Navigator / Communicator
NCO	Non-Commissioned Officer
ND	Negligent Discharge
NDA	National Defence Act
NDHQ	National Defence Headquarters
NPR	National Public Radio
NORAD	North American Aerospáce Defence
NSU	National Support Unit
OC	Officer Commanding
O GP	Orders Group
OP	Observation Post
Op	Operations
OPP	Operational Planning Process
OPSEC	Operational Security
Ops O	Operations Officer
ORBAT	Order of Battle
ORO	Operations Room Officer
PA	Public Affairs
PCO	Privy Council Office
PD	Police District
PIES	proximity; immediacy; expectancy; and simplicity
Pl	Platoon
PM	Prime Minister
PMO	Prime Minister's Office
POE	Point of Entry
PPCLI	Princess Patricia's Canadian Light infantry
PR	Public Relations
PSA	Personnel Support Agency

PSYOPS	Psychological Operations
PTSD	Post Traumatic Stress Disorder
PVO	Private Volunteer Organizations
QRF	Quick Reaction Force
R22eR	Royal 22nd Regiment (R22^{e}R)
Recce	Reconnaissance
RCA	Royal Canadian Artillery
RCHA	Royal Canadian Horse Artillery
RCMP	Royal Canadian Mounted Police
RCR	Royal Canadian Regiment
RM	Rural Municipality
RMC	Royal Military College of Canada
ROE	Rules of Engagement
RPG	Rocket Propelled Grenade
RSK	Republic of Srbska Krijena
RSM	Regimental Sergeant Major
RV	Rendezvous
SACEUR	Supreme Allied Commander Europe
SatCom	Satellite Communications
SEAL	Sea, Land, Air
SFOR	Stabilization Force
SCONSAD	Senate Committee on National Security and Defence
SISIP	Service Income Security Insurance Plan
SITREP	Situation Report
SOF	Special Operations Forces
SOFA	Standard Operating Force Agreement
SOPs	Standard Operating Procedures
SPLA	Sudan People's Liberation Army
SUV	Sport Utility Vehicle
TACNAV	Tactical Navigator
TAL	Tactical Airlift
TCP	Traffic Control Point
TLC	Tender Loving Care
TFMT	Task Force Movement Table
TMST	Theatre Mission Specific Training
TO&E	Table of Organization & Equipment

TOW	Tube Launched, Optically Sited, Wire Guided
TUA	TOW Under Armour
UAE	United Arab Emirates
UK	United Kingdom
UN	United Nations
UNCIVPOL	United Nations Civilian Police
UNHCR	United Nations High Commission on Refugees
UNMO	United Nations Military Observer
UNPA	United Nations Protected Area
UNPROFOR	United Nations Protection Force
UNSCR	United Nations Security Council Resolution
US	United States (of America)
USMC	United States Marine Corps
USN	United States Navy
VCDS	Vice Chief of the Defence Staff
VCP	Vehicle Check Point
VIP	Very Important Person
WO	Warrant Officer
24/7	24 hours a day / seven days a week
2IC	second-in-command

INDEX